Ext JS 4 Plugin and Extension Development

A hands-on development of several Ext JS plugins and extensions

Abdullah Al Mohammad

BIRMINGHAM - MUMBAI

Ext JS 4 Plugin and Extension Development

First published: September 2013

Production Reference: 1130913

Published by Packt Publishing Ltd.
Livery Place
35 Livery Street
Birmingham B3 2PB, UK.

ISBN 978-1-78216-372-5

www.packtpub.com

Cover Image by Suresh Mogre (suresh.mogre.99@gmail.com)

Credits

Author

Abdullah Al Mohammad

Reviewers

Adrian Teodorescu

Li Xudong

Acquisition Editor

Usha Iyer

Commissioning Editor

Neha Nagwekar

Technical Editors

Sampreshita Maheshwari

Menza Mathew

Copy Editor

Sayanee Mukherjee

Alfida Paiva

Adithi Shetty

Laxmi Subraniam

Project Coordinator

Joel Goveya

Proofreader

Lucy Rowland

Indexer

Mariammal Chettiyar

Production Coordinator

Nilesh R. Mohite

Cover Work

Nilesh R. Mohite

About the Author

Abdullah Al Mohammad lives in Rajshahi, Bangladesh. He is a senior freelance software developer having over six years experience. He graduated from Rajshahi University of Engineering and Technology with a B.Sc. in Computer Science and Engineering and began working at HawarIT as a software engineer. He worked there for four years and gained solid experience and then started his career as a freelance developer.

I would like to thank my family, especially my mom and my elder brother, who always provided me with proper guidelines, and my wife for her constant support. I would also like to thank my ex-colleagues from whom I've learned a lot and with whom I've enjoyed working. I would also like to thank Sencha team members as it is because of their hard work I got this loving framework.

About the Reviewers

Adrian Teodorescu is a professional software developer with more than 15 years' experience. Since 2009, Adrian has been devoting most of his time to Sencha libraries, and he is currently focused on building custom components for Ext JS and Sencha Touch. He developed a pivot table for Ext JS, which you can test on his website: www.mzsolutions.eu.

To all the people who believed in me.

Li Xudong is a front-end developer in Beijing, China, and is skilled in JavaScript, CSS, HTML, NodeJS, and Python, and wants to make things better.

www.PacktPub.com

Support files, eBooks, discount offers and more

You might want to visit www.PacktPub.com for support files and downloads related to your book.

Did you know that Packt offers eBook versions of every book published, with PDF and ePub files available? You can upgrade to the eBook version at www.PacktPub.com and as a print book customer, you are entitled to a discount on the eBook copy. Get in touch with us at service@packtpub.com for more details.

At www.PacktPub.com, you can also read a collection of free technical articles, sign up for a range of free newsletters and receive exclusive discounts and offers on Packt books and eBooks.

http://PacktLib.PacktPub.com

Do you need instant solutions to your IT questions? PacktLib is Packt's online digital book library. Here, you can access, read and search across Packt's entire library of books.

Why Subscribe?

- Fully searchable across every book published by Packt
- Copy and paste, print and bookmark content
- On demand and accessible via web browser

Free Access for Packt account holders

If you have an account with Packt at www.PacktPub.com, you can use this to access PacktLib today and view nine entirely free books. Simply use your login credentials for immediate access.

Table of Contents

Preface

In this modern world of JavaScript, Ext JS offers a vast collection of cross-browser utilities, a great collection of UI widgets, charts, data object stores, and much more. When developing an application, we mostly look for the best support for the functionality and components that offer the framework. But we almost always face the situation when the framework does not have the specific functionality or component that we need. Fortunately, Ext JS has a powerful class system that makes it easy to extend an existing functionality or component, or to build new functionalities or components.

In this book, we start by providing a very clear concept of Ext JS plugins and extensions with examples, going through several Ext JS libraries and community-provided plugins and extensions and several hands-on developments of real-life, useful Ext JS plugins and extensions.

What this book covers

Chapter 1, Plugins and Extensions, introduces and defines the Ext JS plugins and extensions, the differences between them, and shows how to develop a plugin and an extension with examples.

Chapter 2, Ext JS-provided Plugins and Extensions, introduces some of the very useful and popular plugins and extensions available within the Ext JS library.

Chapter 3, Ext JS Community Extensions and Plugins, introduces some of the popular Ext JS community extensions and plugins.

Chapter 4, Labeled Spinner, goes through hands-on development of an Ext JS extension called Labeled spinner field. This chapter shows how we can extend the Ext.form.field. Spinner class, and add functionality so that this extension can show a configurable label beside the value within the spinner field and some more advanced features.

Chapter 5, Chart Downloader, goes through hands-on development of an Ext JS plugin, which will help to download a chart as an image. This plugin will generate a button that, when it is clicked, will perform the required functionality so that the plugin container's chart item can be downloaded as an image.

Chapter 6, Grid Search, goes through hands-on development of an Ext JS plugin, which will provide a search facility within a grid. This plugin was originally developed by Ing. Jozef Sakáloš and is a very useful and popular plugin. In this chapter, this plugin will be re-written for the Ext JS 4x Version.

Chapter 7, Input Field with ClearButton, goes through hands-on development of Stephen Friedrich's ClearButton plugin. This plugin is targeted for the text components that show a "clear" button over the text field. When the clear button is clicked, the text field is set to empty.

Chapter 8, Message Bar, goes through hands-on development of an Ext JS extension, which will be a fancy animated message bar. The message bar will provide the facility of having a configurable duration timer for showing the message, a close button, and also be able to customize the look, and can provide optional icons for different types of states such as valid or invalid, or information during runtime.

Chapter 9, Intuitive Multi-select Combobox, explores an excellent Ext JS extension, BoxSelect, which was originally developed by Kevin Vaughan. This extension is really very useful and provides a friendlier combobox for multiple selections, which creates easy and individually removable labels for each selection and lots more.

What you need for this book

The examples in this book use the Ext JS 4.1.3 SDK, available from the Ext JS website at http://www.sencha.com/products/extjs/download.

Who this book is for

The book is aimed at web application developers who are familiar with the basics of Ext JS and want to build custom Ext JS plugins and extensions. Experienced Ext JS developers can also increase their skills in the field of Ext JS plugins and extensions.

Conventions

In this book, you will find a number of styles of text that distinguish between different kinds of information. Here are some examples of these styles, and an explanation of their meaning.

Code words in text are shown as follows: "we will extend the Ext.form.field.Spinner class which will add functionality".

A block of code is set as follows:

```
onSpinUp : function() {
  this.setValue(++this.value);
},

onSpinDown : function() {
  this.setValue(--this.value);
}
```

New terms and **important words** are shown in bold. Words that you see on the screen, in menus or dialog boxes for example, appear in the text like this: "we can find the **Get value** button within the window".

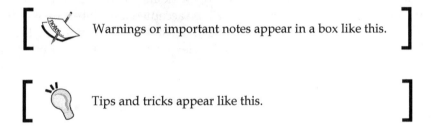

> Warnings or important notes appear in a box like this.

> Tips and tricks appear like this.

Reader feedback

Feedback from our readers is always welcome. Let us know what you think about this book—what you liked or may have disliked. Reader feedback is important for us to develop titles that you really get the most out of.

To send us general feedback, simply send an e-mail to feedback@packtpub.com, and mention the book title via the subject of your message.

If there is a topic that you have expertise in and you are interested in either writing or contributing to a book, see our author guide on www.packtpub.com/authors.

Customer support

Now that you are the proud owner of a Packt book, we have a number of things to help you to get the most from your purchase.

Downloading the example code

You can download the example code files for all Packt books you have purchased from your account at http://www.packtpub.com. If you purchased this book elsewhere, you can visit http://www.packtpub.com/support and register to have the files e-mailed directly to you.

Errata

Although we have taken every care to ensure the accuracy of our content, mistakes do happen. If you find a mistake in one of our books—maybe a mistake in the text or the code—we would be grateful if you would report this to us. By doing so, you can save other readers from frustration and help us improve subsequent versions of this book. If you find any errata, please report them by visiting http://www.packtpub.com/submit-errata, selecting your book, clicking on the **errata submission form** link, and entering the details of your errata. Once your errata are verified, your submission will be accepted and the errata will be uploaded on our website, or added to any list of existing errata, under the Errata section of that title. Any existing errata can be viewed by selecting your title from http://www.packtpub.com/support.

Piracy

Piracy of copyright material on the Internet is an ongoing problem across all media. At Packt, we take the protection of our copyright and licenses very seriously. If you come across any illegal copies of our works, in any form, on the Internet, please provide us with the location address or website name immediately so that we can pursue a remedy.

Please contact us at copyright@packtpub.com with a link to the suspected pirated material.

We appreciate your help in protecting our authors, and our ability to bring you valuable content.

Questions

You can contact us at questions@packtpub.com if you are having a problem with any aspect of the book, and we will do our best to address it.

1
Plugins and Extensions

This chapter introduces and defines the Ext JS plugins and extensions, the differences between them, and finally shows how to develop a plugin and an extension.

In this chapter we will cover:

- What a plugin is
- What an extension is
- Differences between an extension and a plugin, and choosing the best option
- Building an Ext JS plugin
- Building an Ext JS extension

In this modern world of JavaScript, Ext JS is the best JavaScript framework that includes a vast collection of cross-browser utilities, UI widgets, charts, data object stores, and much more.

When developing an application, we mostly look for the best functionality support and components that offer it to the framework. But we usually face situations wherein the framework lacks the specific functionality or component that we need. Fortunately, Ext JS has a powerful class system that makes it easy to extend an existing functionality or component, or build new ones altogether.

What is a plugin?

An Ext JS plugin is a class that is used to provide additional functionalities to an existing component. Plugins must implement a method named init, which is called by the component and is passed as the parameter at the initialization time, at the beginning of the component's lifecycle. The destroy method is invoked by the owning component of the plugin, at the time of the component's destruction. We don't need to instantiate a plugin class. Plugins are inserted in to a component using the plugin's configuration option for that component.

Plugins are used not only by components to which they are attached, but also by all the subclasses derived from that component. We can also use multiple plugins in a single component, but we need to be aware that using multiple plugins in a single component should not let the plugins conflict with each other.

What is an extension?

An Ext JS extension is a derived class or a subclass of an existing Ext JS class, which is designed to allow the inclusion of additional features. An Ext JS extension is mostly used to add custom functionalities or modify the behavior of an existing Ext JS class. An Ext JS extension can be as basic as the preconfigured Ext JS classes, which basically supply a set of default values to an existing class configuration. This type of extension is really helpful in situations where the required functionality is repeated at several places. Let us assume we have an application where several Ext JS windows have the same help button at the bottom bar. So we can create an extension of the Ext JS window, where we can add this help button and can use this extension window without providing the repeated code for the button. The advantage is that we can easily maintain the code for the help button in one place and can get the change in all places.

Differences between an extension and a plugin

The Ext JS extensions and plugins are used for the same purpose; they add extended functionality to Ext JS classes. But they mainly differ in terms of how they are written and the reason for which they are used.

Ext JS extensions are extension classes or subclasses of Ext JS classes. To use these extensions, we need to instantiate these extensions by creating an object. We can provide additional properties, functions, and can even override any parent member to change its behavior. The extensions are very tightly coupled to the classes from which they are derived. The Ext JS extensions are mainly used when we need to modify the behavior of an existing class or component, or we need to create a fully new class or component.

Ext JS plugins are also Ext JS classes, but they include the `init` function. To use the plugins we don't need to directly instantiate these classes; instead, we need to register the plugins in the plugins' configuration option within the component. After adding, the options and functions will become available to the component itself. The plugins are loosely coupled with the components they are plugged in, and they can be easily detachable and interoperable with multiple components and derived components. Plugins are used when we need to add features to a component. As plugins must be attached to an existing component, creating a fully new component, as done in the extensions, is not useful.

Choosing the best option

When we need to enhance or change the functionality of an existing Ext JS component, we have several ways to do that, each of which has both advantages and disadvantages.

Let us assume we need to develop an SMS text field having a simple functionality of changing the text color to red whenever the text length exceeds the allocated length for a message; this way the user can see that they are typing more than one message. Now, this functionality can be implemented in three different ways in Ext JS, which is discussed in the following sections.

By configuring an existing class

We can choose to apply configuration to the existing classes. For example, we can create a text field by providing the required SMS functionality as a configuration within the listener's configuration, or we can provide event handlers after the text field is instantiated with the `on` method.

This is the easiest option when the same functionality is used only at a few places. But as soon as the functionality is repeated at several places or in several situations, code duplication may arise.

By creating a subclass or an extension

By creating an extension, we can easily solve the problem as discussed in the previous section. So, if we create an extension for the SMS text field by extending the Ext JS text field, we can use this extension at as many places as we need, and can also create other extensions by using this extension. So, the code is centralized for this extension, and changing one place can reflect in all the places where this extension is used.

But there is a problem: when the same functionality is needed for SMS in other subclasses of Ext JS text fields such as Ext JS text area field, we can't use the developed SMS text field extension to take advantage of the SMS functionality. Also, assume a situation where there are two subclasses of a base class, each of which provides their own facility, and we want to use both the features on a single class, then it is not possible in this implementation.

By creating a plugin

By creating a plugin, we can gain the maximum re-use of a code. As a plugin for one class, it is usable by the subclasses of that class, and also, we have the flexibility to use multiple plugins in a single component. This is the reason why if we create a plugin for the SMS functionality we can use the SMS plugin both in the text field and in the text area field. Also, we can use other plugins, including this SMS plugin, in the class.

Building an Ext JS plugin

Let us start developing an Ext JS plugin. In this section we will develop a simple SMS plugin, targeting the Ext JS `textareafield` component. The feature we wish to provide for the SMS functionality is that it should show the number of characters and the number of messages on the bottom of the containing field. Also, the color of the text of the message should change in order to notify the users whenever they exceed the allowed length for a message.

Here, in the following code, the SMS plugin class has been created within the `Examples` namespace of an Ext JS application:

```
Ext.define('Examples.plugin.Sms', {

    alias : 'plugin.sms',

    config : {

        perMessageLength : 160,
        defaultColor : '#000000',
        warningColor : '#ff0000'

    },

    constructor : function(cfg) {

        Ext.apply(this, cfg);

        this.callParent(arguments);
    },

    init : function(textField) {
```

```
    this.textField = textField;
    if (!textField.rendered) {
      textField.on('afterrender', this.handleAfterRender, this);
    }
    else {
      this.handleAfterRender();
    }
  },
handleAfterRender : function() {

  this.textField.on({
    scope : this,
    change : this.handleChange
  });

  var dom = Ext.get(this.textField.bodyEl.dom);

  Ext.DomHelper.append(dom, {
    tag : 'div',
    cls : 'plugin-sms'
  });

},

handleChange : function(field, newValue) {

  if (newValue.length > this.getPerMessageLength()) {
    field.setFieldStyle('color:' + this.getWarningColor());
  }
  else {
    field.setFieldStyle('color:' + this.getDefaultColor());
  }
  this.updateMessageInfo(newValue.length);

},

updateMessageInfo : function(length) {

  var tpl = ['Characters: {length}<br/>', 'Messages:
    {messages}'].join('');
  var text = new Ext.XTemplate(tpl);
  var messages = parseInt(length / this.getPerMessageLength());

  if ((length / this.getPerMessageLength()) - messages > 0) {
    ++messages;
  }

  Ext.get(this.getInfoPanel()).update(text.apply({
    length : length,
    messages : messages
  }));
```

```
    },

    getInfoPanel : function() {

        return this.textField.el.select('.plugin-sms');

    }
});
```

Downloading the example code

You can download the example code files for all Packt books you have purchased from your account at http://www.packtpub.com. If you purchased this book elsewhere, you can visit http://www.packtpub.com/support and register to have the files e-mailed directly to you.

In the preceding plugin class, you can see that within this class we have defined a "must implemented" function called `init`. Within the `init` function, we check whether the component, on which this plugin is attached, has rendered or not, and then call the `handleAfterRender` function whenever the rendering is. Within this function, a code is provided, such that when the `change` event fires off the `textareafield` component, the `handleChange` function of this class should get executed; simultaneously, create an HTML `<div>` element within the `handleAfterRender` function, where we want to show the message information regarding the characters and message counter. And the `handleChange` function is the handler that calculates the message length in order to show the colored, warning text, and call the `updateMessageInfo` function to update the message information text for the characters length and the number of messages.

Now we can easily add the following plugin to the component:

```
{
    xtype : 'textareafield',
    plugins : ['sms']
}
```

Also, we can supply configuration options when we are inserting the plugin within the `plugins` configuration option to override the default values, as follows:

```
plugins : [Ext.create('Examples.plugin.Sms', {
    perMessageLength : 20,
    defaultColor : '#0000ff',
    warningColor : "#00ff00"
})]
```

Building an Ext JS extension

Let us start developing an Ext JS extension. In this section we will develop an SMS extension that exactly satisfies the same requirements as the earlier-developed SMS plugin.

We already know that an Ext JS extension is a derived class of existing Ext JS class, we are going to extend the Ext JS's textarea field that facilitates for typing multiline text and provides several event handling, rendering and other functionalities.

Here is the following code where we have created the Extension class under the SMS view within the Examples namespace of an Ext JS application:

```
Ext.define('Examples.view.sms.Extension', {
  extend : 'Ext.form.field.TextArea',
  alias : 'widget.sms',

  config : {

    perMessageLength : 160,
    defaultColor : '#000000',
    warningColor : '#ff0000'

  },

  constructor : function(cfg) {

    Ext.apply(this, cfg);

    this.callParent(arguments);
  },

  afterRender : function() {

    this.on({
      scope : this,
      change : this.handleChange
    });

    var dom = Ext.get(this.bodyEl.dom);

    Ext.DomHelper.append(dom, {
      tag : 'div',
      cls : 'extension-sms'
    });

  },

  handleChange : function(field, newValue) {
```

```
        if (newValue.length > this.getPerMessageLength()) {
          field.setFieldStyle('color:' + this.getWarningColor());
        }
        else {
          field.setFieldStyle('color:' + this.getDefaultColor());
        }
        this.updateMessageInfo(newValue.length);

      },

      updateMessageInfo : function(length) {

        var tpl = ['Characters: {length}<br/>', 'Messages:
          {messages}'].join('');
        var text = new Ext.XTemplate(tpl);
        var messages = parseInt(length / this.getPerMessageLength());

        if ((length / this.getPerMessageLength()) - messages > 0) {
          ++messages;
        }

        Ext.get(this.getInfoPanel()).update(text.apply({
          length : length,
          messages : messages
        }));

      },

      getInfoPanel : function() {

        return this.el.select('.extension-sms');

      }
    });
```

As seen in the preceding code, the `extend` keyword is used as a class property to extend the `Ext.form.field.TextArea` class in order to create the extension class. Within the `afterRender` event handler, we provide a code so that when the `change` event fires off the **textarea** field, we can execute the `handleChange` function of this class and also create an Html `<div>` element within this `afterRender` event handler where we want to show the message information regarding the characters counter and message counter. And from this section, the logic to show the warning, message character counter, and message counter is the same as we used in the SMS plugin.

Now we can easily create an instance of this extension:

```
Ext.create('Examples.view.sms.Extension');
```

Also, we can supply configuration options when we are creating the instance of this class to override the default values:

```
Ext.create('Examples.view.sms.Extension', {
    perMessageLength : 20,
    defaultColor : '#0000ff',
    warningColor : "#00ff00"
});
```

The following is the screenshot where we've used the SMS plugin and extension:

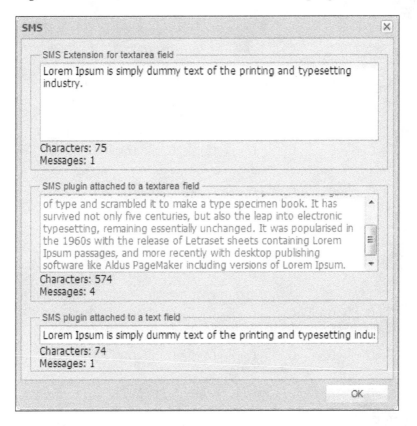

In the above screenshot we have created an Ext JS window and incorporated the SMS extension and SMS plugin. As we have already discussed on the benefit of writing a plugin, we can not only use the SMS plugin with text area field, but we can also use it with text field.

Summary

We have learned from this chapter what a plugin and an extension are, the differences between the two, the facilities they offer, how to use them, and take decisions on choosing either an extension or a plugin for the needed functionality. In this chapter we've also developed a simple SMS plugin and an SMS extension.

2
Ext JS-provided Plugins and Extensions

This chapter introduces some of the very useful and popular plugins and extensions available in the Ext JS library.

In this chapter we will cover:

- MultiSelect
- ItemSelector
- TreeViewDragDrop
- CheckColumn
- CellEditing
- RowEditing
- LiveSearchGridPanel

The MultiSelect extension

`Ext.ux.form.MultiSelect` is a form field type which allows the selection of one or more items from a list. A list is populated using a data store. Items can be reordered via the drag-and-drop method, if the `ddReorder` property of this class is set to `true`.

Here, in the following code, a form panel class has been defined, in which the `MultiSelect` extension has been used as an item of this form:

```
Ext.define('Examples.view.multiselect.MultiSelectFormPanel', {
  extend : 'Ext.form.Panel',
  alias : 'widget.multiselectformpanel',
  requires : ['Ext.ux.form.MultiSelect'],

  constructor : function(config) {

    Ext.apply(this, {
      bodyPadding : 10,
      items : [{
        anchor : '100%',
        xtype : 'multiselect',
        fieldLabel : 'Multi Select',
        name : 'multiselect',
        store : Ext.create('Examples.store.DummyStore'),
        valueField : 'name',
        displayField : 'name',
        ddReorder : true,
        listeners : {
          change : {
            fn : this.getMultiSelectValue
          },
          scope : this
        }
      }]
    });
    this.callParent(arguments);

  },

  getMultiSelectValue : function() {
    var title = "Multiselect values",
    value = this.getForm().findField('multiselect').getValue();
    Ext.Msg.alert(title, value);
  }
});
```

You can see in the preceding code that the `ddReorder` option is set to `true` in order to reorder the items by the drag-and-drop method. And also, by using the `getMultiSelectValue` function as the `change` event handler of the `multiselect` field, a message, with the selected value of the `multiselect` field, can be displayed.

In the following screenshot, you can see the result of the `MultiSelectFormPanel` class that we have defined, which is used within a window:

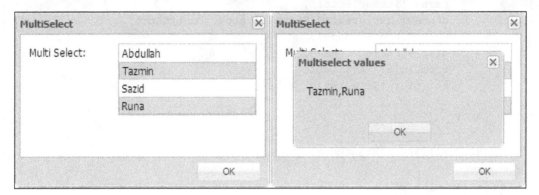

You can see that we can select multiple values, and as soon as we select the items in the list, the selected values of the multiselect field is shown as the message, the selected value of the `multiselect` field is shown as the message.

The available configuration options, properties, methods, and events for this extension is documented at `http://docs.sencha.com/extjs/4.1.3/#!/api/Ext.ux.form.MultiSelect`.

The ItemSelector extension

`ItemSelector` is a specialized `MultiSelect` field that renders as a pair with the `MultiSelect` field; one with the available options and the other with the selected options. A set of buttons in between, allows the items to be moved between the fields and reordered within the selection. Also, they can be moved via drag-and-drop method.

Here, in the following code, a form panel class is defined, in which we are using the `ItemSelector` extension as an item of this form:

```
Ext.define('Examples.view.itemselector.ItemSelectorFormPanel', {
    extend : 'Ext.form.Panel',
    alias : 'widget.itemselectorformpanel',
    requires : ['Ext.ux.form.ItemSelector'],
```

```
constructor : function(config) {

  Ext.apply(this, {
    bodyPadding : 10,
    items : [{
      anchor : '100%',
      xtype: 'itemselector',
      name: 'itemselector',
      store : Ext.create('Examples.store.DummyStore'),
      valueField : 'name',
      displayField : 'name',
      fromTitle: 'Available',
      toTitle: 'Selected'

    }]
  });
  this.callParent(arguments);

  }
});
```

You can see in the following screenshot that the ItemSelector extension is a pair of MultiSelect field where one is loaded with data store:

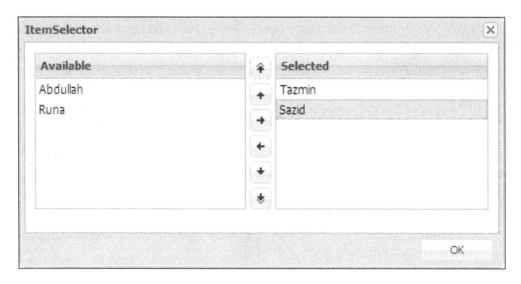

We can select the values from this available field and can move those values to the **Selected** field. We can use the arrow buttons or drag-and-drop, to move the values within those fields or reorder between those. If we use the `getValue` function of this `ItemSelector` extension, it will return the collection of values available at the **Selected** field.

The documentation for this extension is available at `http://docs.sencha.com/extjs/4.1.3/#!/api/Ext.ux.form.ItemSelector`, where you will get all the available configuration options, properties, methods, and events for this extension.

The TreeViewDragDrop plugin

This plugin provides a drag and/or drop functionality for a `TreeView` class. It creates a specialized instance of `DragZone`, which knows how to drag out of a `TreeView` class, and loads the data object which is passed on to the cooperating methods of `DragZone` with the following properties:

- **copy**: `Boolean`

  It is the value of the `copy` property of `TreeView` or `true` if the `TreeView` class was configured with `allowCopy` set to `true` and the *Ctrl* key was pressed when the drag operation was begun.

- **view**: `TreeView`

  It is the source `TreeView` from which the drag originated.

- **ddel**: `HtmlElement`

  It is the drag proxy element which moves with the mouse.

- **item**: `HtmlElement`

  It is the `TreeView` node upon which the `mousedown` event was registered.

- **records**: `Array`

  It is an array of models representing the selected data being dragged from the source `TreeView`.

It also creates a specialized instance of Ext.dd.DropZone, which cooperates with other DropZone classes. These DropZone classes are members of the same ddGroup, which processes such data objects. Adding this plugin to a view means that two new events may be fired from the client TreeView, before the drag-and-drop.

> Note that the plugin must be added to the tree view, and not to the tree panel. For example, by using viewConfig:
> ```
> viewConfig: {
>     plugins: { ptype: 'treeviewdragdrop' }
> }
> ```

Here, in the following code snippet, a tree class has been defined, in which the TreeViewDragDrop plugin is used to drag-and-drop the nodes:

```
Ext.define('Examples.view.treeviewdragdrop.TreeViewDragDropTree', {
    extend : 'Ext.tree.Panel',
    alias : 'widget.treeviewdragdroptree',
    requires : ['Examples.store.SampleTreeStore',
                'Ext.tree.plugin.TreeViewDragDrop'],

    constructor : function(config) {

        Ext.apply(this, {
            border : false,
            store : Ext.create('Examples.store.SampleTreeStore'),
            viewConfig : {
                plugins : [
                    'treeviewdragdrop'
                ]
            },
            useArrows : true
        });

        this.callParent(arguments);

    }
});
```

In the following screenshot you can see the result of the `TreeViewDragDropTree` class that we have defined, which is used within a window:

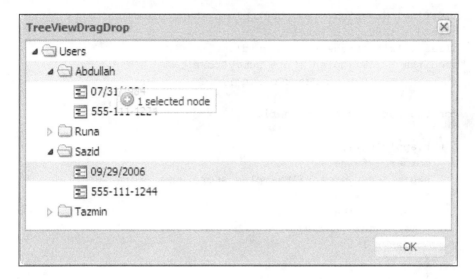

You can see that when we are dragging the **09/29/2006** node, a visible floating message stating that one node is selected, is shown, and then we can easily drop that node within other nodes.

This plugin is well documented at `http://docs.sencha.com/extjs/4.1.3/#!/` `api/Ext.tree.plugin.TreeViewDragDrop`, where you will get all the available configuration options, properties, methods, and events for this plugin.

The CheckColumn extension

`Ext.ux.CheckColumn` is an extension of `Ext.grid.column.Column` that renders a checkbox in each column cell. This checkbox toggles the truthiness of the associated data field on a click. In addition to toggling a Boolean value within the record data, this class adds or removes a CSS class `x-grid-checked`, on the `<td>` element based on whether or not it is checked to alter the background image used for a column.

Here in the following code we are defining a grid class in which we are using the CheckColumn extension to provide a checkbox within each cell of a column:

```
Ext.define('Examples.view.checkcolumn.CheckColumnGrid', {
  extend : 'Ext.grid.Panel',
  alias : 'widget.checkcolumngrid',
  requires : ['Examples.store.DummyStore',
              'Ext.ux.CheckColumn'],

  constructor : function(config) {

    Ext.apply(this, {
      border : false,
      store : Ext.create('Examples.store.DummyStore'),
      columns : [{
        header : 'Name',
        dataIndex : 'name',
        flex : 1
      },
      {
        header : 'Birth date',
        dataIndex : 'birthdate',
        renderer : Ext.util.Format.dateRenderer('m/d/Y')
      },
      {
        xtype : 'checkcolumn',
        header : 'Attending?',
        dataIndex : 'attending'
      }]

    });

    this.callParent(arguments);

  }
});
```

Here, in the following screenshot, you can see the result of the `CheckColumnGrid` class that we have defined which is used within a window:

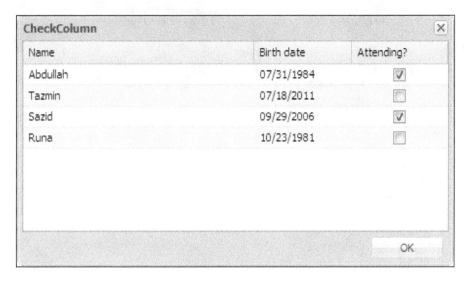

You can see the **Attending?** column, where the `CheckColumn` extension has generated the checkboxes that use the store values to determine whether the checkbox should be checked or not.

The available configuration options, properties, methods, and events for this extension is documented at `http://docs.sencha.com/extjs/4.1.3/#!/api/Ext.ux.CheckColumn`.

The CellEditing plugin

The `Ext.grid.plugin.CellEditing` plugin injects editing at the cell level for a Grid. The `editor` field can be a field instance or a field configuration which needs to be provided within the `editor` configuration option within the `columns` definition. With the `CellEditing` plugin we can edit a cell at any time. If an editor is not specified for a particular column, that cell cannot be edited and it will be skipped when activated via the mouse or the keyboard.

When we configure a column to use an editor for cell editing, we should choose an appropriate field type to match the data type that this editor field will be editing. For example, to edit a date value in the cell, it would be useful to specify `Ext.form.field.Date` as the editor.

Here, in the following code we are defining a grid class in which we are using the
CellEditing plugin to edit the cells:

```
Ext.define('Examples.view.cellediting.CellEditingGrid', {
  extend : 'Ext.grid.Panel',
  alias : 'widget.celleditingGrid',
  requires : ['Examples.store.DummyStore',
              'Ext.grid.plugin.CellEditing',
              'Ext.form.field.Date'],

  constructor : function(config) {

    Ext.apply(this, {
      store : Ext.create('Examples.store.DummyStore'),
      columns : [{
        header : 'Name',
        dataIndex : 'name',
        flex : 1,
        editor : 'textfield'
      },
      {
        header : 'Birth date',
        dataIndex : 'birthdate',
        renderer : Ext.util.Format.dateRenderer('m/d/Y'),
        flex : 1,
        editor : {
          xtype : 'datefield',
          allowBlank : false
        }
      }],
      selType : 'cellmodel',
      plugins : [Ext.create('Ext.grid.plugin.CellEditing', {
        clicksToEdit : 1
      })]
    });

    this.callParent(arguments);

  }
});
```

You can see in the code that in the `columns` definition, the `editor` configuration has been provided with the `textfield` option to edit the **Name** cells and the `datefield` option to edit the **Birth date** cells. To support cell editing, it's specified that the grid should use the `cellmodel` option for `selType`, and create an instance of the `CellEditing` plugin. The plugin has been configured to activate each editor after a single click, by setting the `clicksToEdit` configuration option to 1. The value can be set to 2 too, for the `clicksToEdit` option to activate the editor by double-click. There is another configuration option called `triggerEvent`, which also triggers the editing, and supercedes the `clicksToEdit` configuration option. The value for `triggerEvent` option can be set to `cellclick`, `celldblclick`, `cellfocus`, and `rowfocus`.

Here, in the following screenshot you can see the result of the `CellEditingGrid` class that we have defined which is used within a window:

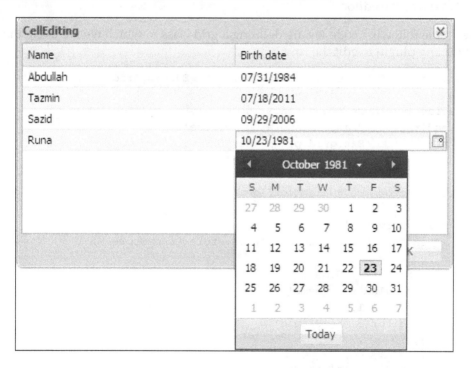

You can see that a date field allows you to choose a date from a date picker as soon as the cell is clicked.

This plugin is well documented at `http://docs.sencha.com/extjs/4.1.3/#!/api/Ext.grid.plugin.CellEditing`, where you will get all the available configuration options, properties, methods, and events for this plugin.

The RowEditing plugin

The `Ext.grid.plugin.RowEditing` plugin injects editing at the row level for a Grid. When editing begins, a small floating dialog will be shown for the appropriate row. Each editable column will show a field for editing. There is a button to save or cancel all changes for the edit. The `editor` field can be a field instance or a field configuration and we need to provide this within the `editor` configuration option within the column definition. If an editor is not specified for a particular column, the cell of that column will not be editable and the value of the cell will be displayed.

When we configure a column to use an editor for row editing, we should choose an appropriate field type to match the data type that this editor field will be editing. For example, to edit a date value in the cell, it would be useful to specify `Ext.form.field.Date` as the editor.

Here, in the following code we are defining a grid class in which we are using the `RowEditing` plugin to edit the row:

```
Ext.define('Examples.view.rowediting.RowEditingGrid',{
  extend : 'Ext.grid.Panel',
  alias : 'widget.roweditingGrid',
  requires : ['Examples.store.DummyStore',
              'Ext.grid.plugin.RowEditing',
              'Ext.form.field.Date'],

  constructor : function(config) {

    Ext.apply(this, {
      store : Ext.create('Examples.store.DummyStore'),
      columns : [{
        header : 'Name',
        dataIndex : 'name',
        flex : 1,
        editor : 'textfield'
      },
      {
        header : 'Birth date',
        dataIndex : 'birthdate',
        renderer : Ext.util.Format.dateRenderer('m/d/Y'),
        flex : 1,
        editor : {
          xtype : 'datefield',
          allowBlank : false
        }
      }],
```

```
      selType : 'rowmodel',
      plugins : [Ext.create('Ext.grid.plugin.RowEditing',{
        clicksToEdit : 1
      })]
    });

    this.callParent(arguments);


  }
});
```

You can see in the code that in the `columns` definition, the `editor` configuration has been provided with the `textfield` option to edit the **Name** cells and the `datefield` option to edit the **Birth date** cells. To support row editing, it's specified that the grid should use `rowmodel` as the value for the `selType` configuration. An instance of the `RowEditing` plugin has been created, which has been configured to activate each editor after a single click.

In the following screenshot you can see the result of the `RowEditing` grid class that we have defined which is used within a window:

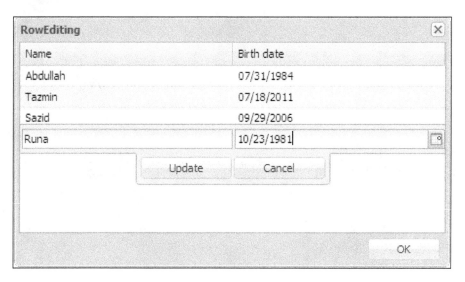

You can see that a floating dialog is showing just on top of the editing row with the provided editors including the **Update** and **Cancel** buttons.

The available configuration options, properties, methods, and events for this plug-in is documented at `http://docs.sencha.com/extjs/4.1.3/#!/api/Ext.grid.plugin.RowEditing`.

The LiveSearchGridPanel extension

`Ext.ux.LiveSearchGridPanel` is a `GridPanel` class that supports live search.

Here, in the following code, a grid panel class is defined by extending the `LiveSearchGridPanel` extension:

```
Ext.define('Examples.view.livesearch.LiveSearchGrid', {
    extend : 'Ext.ux.LiveSearchGridPanel',
    alias : 'widget.livesearchgrid',
    requires : ['Examples.store.DummyStore'],

    constructor : function(config) {

        Ext.apply(this, {
            border : false,
            store : Ext.create('Examples.store.DummyStore'),
            columns : [{
                header : 'Name',
                dataIndex : 'name',
                flex : 1
            },
            {
                header : 'Birth date',
                dataIndex : 'birthdate',
                renderer : Ext.util.Format.dateRenderer('m/d/Y'),
                flex : 1
            }]
        });

        this.callParent(arguments);

    }
});
```

In the following screenshot you can see the result of the `LiveSearchGrid` class that we have defined, which is used within a window:

You can see that a grid panel with a **Search** input box, previous and next buttons, **Regular expression**, and **Case sensitive** options, and a status bar for proper messaging is generated. This extension, `GridPanel`, highlights the matched text and selects the first row of the matched text rows. Then we can also use the previous and next buttons to move the selection between those rows.

The documentation for this extension is available at `http://docs.sencha.com/extjs/4.1.3/#!/api/Ext.ux.LiveSearchGridPanel`, where all the available configuration options, properties, methods, and events for this extension is documented.

Summary

Ext JS is really a rich library that provides several ready-to-use, useful extensions and plugins. In this chapter we went through some of those popular extensions and plugins, and learned how to use them.

In the next chapter we will go through hands-on development of an extension called Labeled Spinner by extending the `Ext.form.field.Spinner` class.

3
Ext JS Community Extensions and Plugins

The Ext JS Community has a rich collection of extensions and plugins. This chapter introduces us to some of the popular extensions and plugins of Ext JS Community.

In this chapter we will cover:

- Callout
- SmartLegend
- TitleChart
- BoxSelect
- MultiDate
- MultiMonth
- MultiSelect
- TinyMCETextArea
- FilterBar
- DragSelector

The Callout extension

Callout is an extension class, which is a CSS styleable floating callout container with an optional arrow, developed by John Yanarella. It is useful for creating hint overlays and interactive callout windows/popovers.

We can see a `callout` popover in the following screenshot:

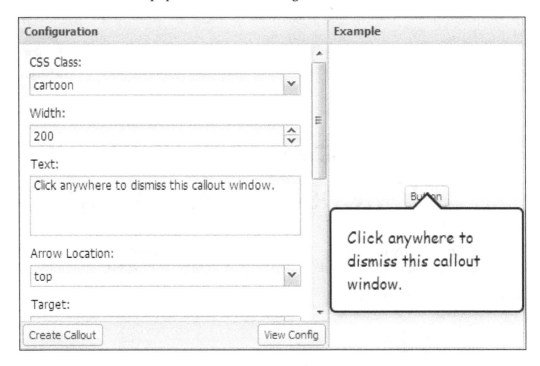

An `Ext.ux.callout.Callout` extension can be easily configured to:

- Show its associated callout arrow at various locations, including top, bottom, left, right, top-left, top-right, bottom-left, bottom-right, left-top, left-bottom, right-top, right-bottom

- Position itself relative to a target `Ext.Element` or `Ext.Component`, and it will maintain that relative position when that target moves or the browser resizes

- Automatically hides itself in response to mouse clicks outside the callout bounds

- Automatically dismisses itself after a configurable delay

- Fade in when shown, and fade out when hidden

A live demo is available for this extension at `http://lab.codecatalyst.com/Ext. ux.callout.Callout`. This extension is licensed under **Massachusetts Institute of Technology (MIT)**. The download link, details of the copyright, and license for this extension are available at `https://github.com/CodeCatalyst/Ext. ux.callout.Callout`.

The SmartLegend extension

SmartLegend is an extension which implements the chart legend with a more advanced behavior, developed by Alexander Tokarev. This extension class is basically the same as Ext.chart.Legend, except that some of its methods were refactored for a better re-use.

Following is the screenshot of a chart where the SmartLegend extension is used:

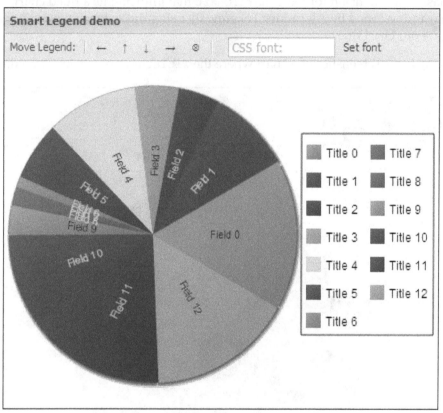

The following are some of the features of SmartLegend:

- The sizes of legend items are adjusted to the font size
- Legend items can be configured to display any particular text, not only fixed series titles or values
- Legend draws itself in several rows or columns, depending on the orientation

A live demo for this extension is located at http://nohuhu.org/demos/demo_ smartlegend.html.This extension is licensed under GPLv3. The download link, details of the copyright, and license for this extension are available at https://github.com/nohuhu/Ext.ux.chart.SmartLegend.

The TitleChart extension

This class is an extension for Ext.chart.Chart that implements a titled chart, which was developed by Alexander Tokarev. By using this extension we can easily configure our chart title.

Following is the screenshot of a chart where the TitleChart extension is used:

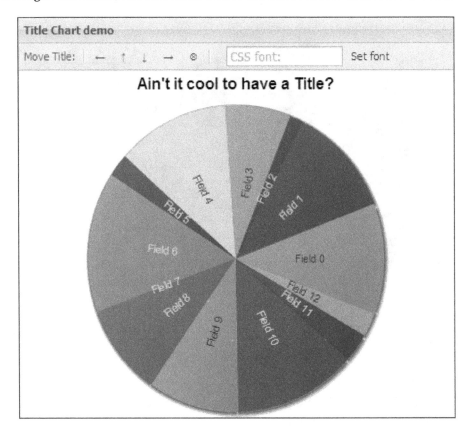

The available configuration options are:

- **titleLocation**: `left`, `right`, `top` or `bottom`. The title text will be rotated accordingly when location is right or left.
- **titleFont**: The font properties for chart title, in CSS format.
- **titlePadding**: The space between chart canvas edge and title, in pixels.
- **titleMargin**: The space between title and actual chart area.

A live demo for this extension is located at `http://nohuhu.org/demos/demo_titlechart.html`. This extension is licensed under GPLv3. The download link, details of the copyright, and license for this extension are available at `https://github.com/nohuhu/Ext.ux.chart.TitleChart`.

The BoxSelect extension

`Ext.ux.form.field.BoxSelect` is a combobox, extended for more intuitive multiselect capabilities using individually labeled selected items, developed by Kevin Vaughan.

In the following screenshot you can see how multiple items are selected within a `BoxSelect` combobox:

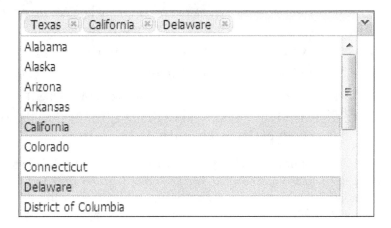

In the following screenshot you can see how the selected values and the dropdowns are both configured via templates:

The following are some of the features of `BoxSelect`:

- Individually removable labeled items for each selected value.

- Customizable item templates, in addition to combobox's support of customizable drop-down list templates.

- Keyboard-based selection and navigation of selected values (left/right, *Shift*, *Ctrl* + *A*, *Backspace*, *Delete*).

- On-demand loading of values from remote stores when an unknown value is set, that is, setting `queryMode = 'remote'` and `forceSelection = true`.

- Creation of new value records for `forceSelection = false`.

- Configurable pinning of combo pick list for `multiSelect = true`.

- Configurable rendering of labeled items (auto-sized or stacked).

- As `BoxSelect` extends ComboBox, most (if not all) of the functionality and configuration options of ComboBox should work as expected.

This extension is licensed under MIT. Examples and reference for this extension are available at `http://kveeiv.github.io/extjs-boxselect/examples/boxselect.html`. The download link, details of the copyright, and license for this extension are available at `https://github.com/kveeiv/extjs-boxselect`.

The MultiDate extension

`MultiDate` is a form field extension, which is extended from `Ext.form.field.Date`, which allows entering of multiple dates and date ranges with flexible format-matching and powerful drop-down picker, developed by Alexander Tokarev.

Following is the screenshot of a `MultiDate` field:

The following are some of the features for `MultiDate`:

- No limit for number of dates or date ranges.
- Separate settings for input format, display format, and submit format of range values.
- Fully themed with CSS sheet provided.
- Backwards compatibility: multivalue input can be turned off by setting one option; in this case, behavior is similar to the **stockDate** field.
- Support for configurable work weekdays selection.
- Press *Space* in picker to select/unselect single day.
- *Shift* + *Space* or *Shift* + click in picker selects the work week.
- *Ctrl* + *Backspace* in picker clears the selection.
- *Ctrl* + click in picker selects the freeform ranges: *Ctrl* + click once to set the start date and *Ctrl* + click again to set the end date and select all dates in between. This works across several months/years too.

- *Ctrl* + *Shift* + click in picker selects freeform ranges but includes only work days.
- Press *Enter* in picker to confirm the selection.
- Press *Esc* in picker to cancel the selection.

A live demo for this extension is located at `http://nohuhu.org/demos/demo_uxmultidate.html`. This extension is licensed under GPLv3. The download link, details of the copyright, and license for this extension are available at `https://github.com/nohuhu/Ext.ux.form.field.MultiDate`.

The MultiMonth extension

`MultiMonth` is a form field extension that allows entering month ranges, with flexible format matching and customized drop-down picker, developed by Alexander Tokarev.

Following is the screenshot of a `MultiMonth` field:

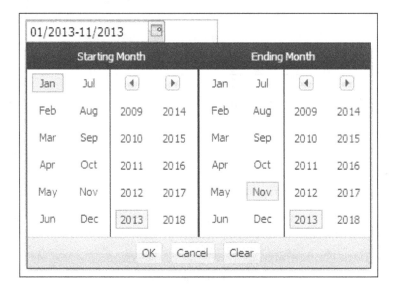

The following are some of the features of `MultiMonth`:

- Allows the entering of starting and ending months
- Separate settings for input format, display, and submit formats
- Fully themed with CSS sheet provided
- Switched behavior: set `multiValue` property to `false` and the field will allow only single month to be entered

A live demo for this extension is located at `http://nohuhu.org/demos/ demo_uxmultimonth.html`. This extension is licensed under GPLv3. The download link, details of the copyright, and license for this extension are available at `https://github.com/nohuhu/Ext.ux.form.field.MultiDate`.

The MultiSelect extension

`MultiSelect` is a form field for entering the values and value ranges of arbitrary type, with drop-down picker featuring live search with smart matching, visual selection, and more, developed by Alexander Tokarev.

The following is the screenshot of a `MultiSelect` field:

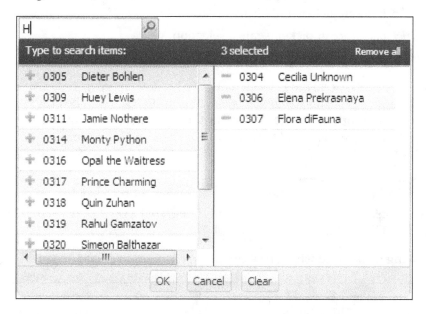

This extension implements a form field that allows the entering of multiple values and value ranges of arbitrary type, with drop-down picker that provides live search and visual item selection.

Following are some of the features of `MultiSelect`:

- No limit for the number of items and item ranges.
- Separate settings for input format, display format, and submit format of single and range values.
- Fully themed form field with CSS sheet provided.
- Two modes of operation: multiple values and single value.

- Drop-down picker with live search and smart matching.
- Optimized for large datasets.
- Accepts preconfigured stores with the list of values to display.
- Supports lazy store population; data is loaded only when a picker is activated.
- Configurable column definition; no arbitrary limit on number and width of columns.
- Press *Enter* in picker or click on the plus icon to select single items.
- Press *Tab* to select a list and press *Enter*, or click on the minus icon to unselect an item.
- *Ctrl + Enter* in picker confirms a selection.
- *Ctrl + Backspace* in picker clears a selection.
- *Esc* in picker to cancel a selection.

A live demo for this extension is located at `http://nohuhu.org/demos/demo_uxmultiselect.html`. This extension is licensed under GPLv3. The download link, details of the copyright, and license for this extension are available at `https://github.com/nohuhu/Ext.ux.form.field.MultiSelect`.

The TinyMCETextArea extension

`TinyMCETextArea` is an Ext JS text area with integrated `TinyMCE` WYSIWYG Editor, developed by Oleg Schildt.

The following is the screenshot of a `TinyMCETextArea` text area:

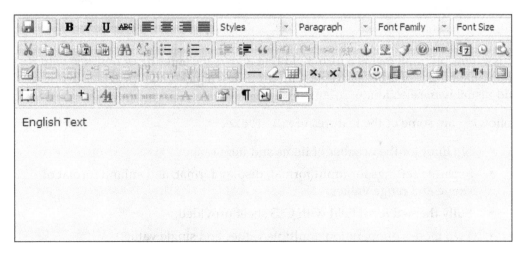

A live demo for this extension is located at `http://www.point-constructor.com/tinyta_demo`. This extension is licensed under GPLv3. You can download this extension at `https://market.sencha.com/extensions/ext-ux-form-tinymcetextarea/versions/2.6/download`.

The FilterBar plugin

`FilterBar` is a plugin that enables filters on the grid headers, developed by ldonofrio.

The following is the screenshot of a grid where the `FilterBar` plugin is used:

#	Price	% Change	Last Updated	Category	
1	$71.72	0.03%	09/01/2013	Category 1	
2	$29.01	1.47%	09/01/2013	Category 2	
3	$83.81	0.34%	09/01/2013	Category 3	
4	$52.55	0.02%	09/01/2013	Category 4	
5	$64.13	0.49%	09/01/2013	Category 5	
6	$31.61	-1.54%	09/01/2013	Category 6	
7	$75.43	0.71%	09/01/2013	Category 1	
8	$67.27	1.39%	09/01/2013	Category 1	
9	$49.37	0.04%	09/01/2013	Category 7	
10	$40.48	1.28%	09/01/2013	Category 1	
11	$68.10	-0.64%	09/01/2013	Category 1	
12	$34.14	-0.23%	09/01/2013	Category 2	

Array Grid

Here are some of the features of the `FilterBar` plugin:

- Allows preconfigured filter's types and auto-based on-store field data types
- Conditional operator selection for better query
- Autogenerated stores for combo and list filters (local collect or server in `autoStoresRemoteProperty` response property)
- Supports the `clearAll` and `showHide` buttons rendered in an action column or in new generated small column

This plugin is licensed under GPLv3. The download link for this plugin is available at `https://market.sencha.com/extensions/ext-ux-grid-filterbar/versions/218/download`.

The DragSelector plugin

`DragSelector` is a plugin that helps selecting grid rows by dragging the mouse over the rows, developed by Harald Hanek. The initial developer of the original code is Claudio Walser. This plugin is really helpful as it supports selecting multiple rows very quickly. It supports the selection of grid rows in the following ways:

- Selecting by dragging over the rows
- Press the *Ctrl* key and select by dragging, keeping the existing selections
- Press the *Ctrl* key and deselect the existing selections, by intersecting the existing selections by dragging the mouse.

In the following screenshot, we can see the `DragSelector` plugin in action:

A live demo for this plugin is located at `http://harrydeluxe.github.io/extjs-ux/example/grid/dragselector.html`. This plugin is licensed under LGPLv3. You can download this plugin at `https://github.com/harrydeluxe/extjs-ux/blob/master/ux/grid/plugin/DragSelector.js`.

Summary

In this chapter, we went through some of the popular Ext JS community extensions and plugins. There are a lot of Ext JS community extensions and plugins, out of which we may find our required ones; and day by day the community extensions and plugins are growing.

4
Labeled Spinner

In this chapter we are going to develop an Ext JS extension called **Labeled spinner**. To develop this extension, we will extend the Ext.form.field.Spinner class, which will add a functionality that will show a configurable label besides the value within the spinner field, and some more advanced features.

In this chapter we will cover:

- Functional requirements
- Planning and coding the labeled spinner

Functional requirements

We want to develop a field for numeric values which will provide the facility of having up/down spinner buttons to increase or decrease the numeric values. Also, a user can edit the value within the field. There will also be a configuration option to show a user-defined label as a unit name just beside the numeric value within the field. There will also be options to get the value from this field, which will be just the numeric value and also the numeric value including the unit name exactly as it shows within the field.

Planning and coding the labeled spinner

To meet the functional requirements, we will create an extension class by extending the Ext JS's `Ext.form.field.Spinner` class from which we will get most of the facilities that we need to provide. We need to implement the `onSpinUp` and `onSpinDown` functions of the `Ext.form.field.Spinner` class to handle the spinner button click event to provide our logic to increase or decrease the values. By default, pressing the up and down arrow keys will also trigger the `onSpinUp` and `onSpinDown` methods. Now, let us start coding:

```
Ext.define('Examples.ux.LabeledSpinner', {
   extend : 'Ext.form.field.Spinner',
   alias : 'widget.labeledspinner',

   onSpinUp : function() {
     this.setValue(++this.value);
   },

   onSpinDown : function() {
     this.setValue(--this.value);
   }
});
```

And now we have a working extension that can increase or decrease its value. Here is the screenshot where we used this extension:

You can see that we now have a field with up/down spinner buttons with which we can increase or decrease the value by 1.

Now, we will add a functionality that this field can show the unit label text just beside the numeric value. We will define the `setValue` function from which we can set the value including the label unit. We will also add some `config` properties to this class so that we can set the values as we needed:

```
Ext.define('Examples.ux.LabeledSpinner', {
    extend : 'Ext.form.field.Spinner',
    alias : 'widget.labeledspinner',

    config : {
        labelText : ",
        minValue: 0,
        value: 0
    },

    onSpinUp : function() {
        var value = parseFloat(this.getValue().split(' ')[0]);
        this.setValue(++value);
    },

    onSpinDown : function() {
        var value = parseFloat(this.getValue().split(' ')[0]);
        this.setValue(--value);
    },

    setValue : function(value) {
        value = (value ||this.minValue) + ' ' +this.getLabelText();
        this.callParent(arguments);
    }
});
```

In the following screenshot, we can see the label just beside the numeric value within the field:

Within the code, you can find that we have provided some `config` options, added the `setValue` function, and modified a little of the `onSpinUp` and `onSpinDown` functions.

Now, we will define the `getValue` function so that we can get the numeric value from this field and define the `getLabeledValue` function that will return the numeric value, including the unit label, exactly as it shows on the field. We will also define the `onBlur` handler to check and fix it with a minimum value, if there is any wrong input and will do some changes on the existing code. Here is the complete code for our extension:

```
Ext.define('Examples.ux.LabeledSpinner', {
  extend : 'Ext.form.field.Spinner',
  alias : 'widget.labeledspinner',

  config : {
    labelText : '',
    minValue : 0,
    maxValue : Number.MAX_VALUE,
    step : 1,
    value : 0
  },

  onBlur : function() {
    if (isNaN(this.getValue())) {
      this.setValue(this.getLabeledValue(this.getMinValue()));
    }
    else{
      this.setValue(this.getLabeledValue());
    }
  },

  onSpinUp : function() {
    var val = this.getValue() || this.getMinValue();
    this.setChangedValue(val + this.step);
  },

  onSpinDown : function() {
    var val = this.getValue() || this.getMinValue();

    this.setChangedValue(val - this.step);
  },

  getLabeledValue : function(value) {
    value = Ext.isDefined(value) ? value : this.getValue();
    if (value.toString().indexOf(this.getLabelText()) == -1) {
      return value + ' ' + this.getLabelText();
    } else {
      return value;
    }
```

```
    },

    setValue : function(value) {
      if(!this.readOnly){
        value = this.getLabeledValue(value);
      }
      this.callParent(arguments);
    },

    getValue : function() {
      var me = this,
      val = me.rawToValue(me.processRawValue(me.getRawValue()));

      val = parseFloat(val.split(' ')[0]);
      return val;
    },

    setChangedValue : function(value){
      if(!isNaN(value)){
        this.setValue(Ext.Number.constrain(value,
          this.getMinValue(), this.getMaxValue()));
      }
    }
  }

});
```

And following is the screenshot of our working **LabeledSpinner** extension:

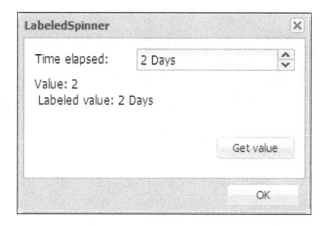

In the preceding screenshot, we can find the **Get value** button within the window. When this button is clicked, we print the values on the window by calling both the getValue and getLabeledValue functions.

Summary

In this chapter, we've developed a new component by extending Ext JS's existing class and we've learned how we can easily create Ext JS extensions and inject our required functionality. In the next chapter, we will develop an Ext JS plugin called the Chart download, which generates a button on the container's toolbar and can download the container's chart item as an image when this button is clicked.

5
Chart Downloader

In this chapter we are going to develop an Ext JS plugin, which will help us to download a chart as an image. This plugin will generate a button and when the button is clicked, it will perform the required functionality, such that the plugin container's chart item will be downloaded as an image.

In this chapter we will cover:

- Functional requirements
- Planning and coding the chart downloader

Functional requirements

We want to develop a plugin that will facilitate downloading a chart as an image. The plugin will generate a button at the container's bottom toolbar. If the container does not contain any toolbar at the bottom, this plugin should create a bottom toolbar for the container and then it will generate the button within the toolbar. When this button is clicked, the plugin will search for a chart item within the container and will download the chart as an image.

Planning and coding the chart downloader

The plugin's container may or may not have the bottom bar, so we need to search for the bottom bar within the container. If found, we will use that, otherwise we need to create the bottom bar, and then we can add the download button to that bottom bar.

Now let us start coding for the plugin.

```
Ext.define('Examples.plugin.ChartDownload', {

    alias : 'plugin.chartdownload',

    config : {
      chartXtype: 'chart',
      downloadButtonText: 'Download as image',
      chartNotFoundErrorMsg: 'No valid chart type found!',
      errorText: 'Error'
    }
...
```

Here we are providing a configuration option `chartXtype` so that we can configure this plugin with a proper xtype of the chart, which we are targeting to download as an image. Now let us define the required `init` function for this plugin:

```
init : function(container) {

    this.container = container;

    if (!container.rendered) {
      container.on('afterrender', this.handleAfterRender, this);
    } else {
      this.handleAfterRender();
    }

}
```

And now let us define the `handleAfterRender` function:

```
handleAfterRender : function(container) {

    this.chart = this.container.down(this.getChartXtype());

    if(!Ext.isDefined(this.chart) || this.chart ==null){
      Ext.Function.defer(function(){
        this.showErrorMessage({
          title: this.getErrorText(),
          text: this.getChartNotFoundErrorMsg()
        })
      }, 1000, this);
    }

    else{

      this.addDownloadButton();
    }

},
```

In this function, we are trying to get the chart component, and if the chart component isn't found, we will show an error message. And if the chart component is found, we will call the addDownloadButton function, which will create and add the download button. Now let us define the addDownloadButton function:

```
addDownloadButton: function(){

  var toolbar = this.getToolbar(),
  itemsToAdd = [],
  placeholder = '->',
  button = {
    iconCls : 'icon-export',
    text : this.getDownloadButtonText(),
    handler: this.saveChart,
    scope : this
  };

  if(toolbar.items.items.length === 0){
    itemsToAdd.push(placeholder);
  }

  itemsToAdd.push(button);
  toolbar.add(itemsToAdd);
}
```

In this function, first we are trying to get the bottom toolbar by calling the getToolbar function and then adding the download button to that toolbar. Now let us define the getToolbar function:

```
getToolbar: function(){

  var dockedItems = this.container.getDockedItems(),
  toolbar = null,
  hasToolbar = false;

  if(dockedItems.length>0){
    Ext.each(dockedItems, function(item){
      if(item.xtype ==='toolbar' && item.dock == 'bottom'){
        hasToolbar = true;
        toolbar = item;
        return false;
      }
    });
  }
```

```
  if(!hasToolbar){
    toolbar = this.container.addDocked({
      xtype: 'toolbar',
      dock: 'bottom'
    })[0];
  }

  return toolbar;

}
```

You can see that in this function we are trying to get the container's bottom toolbar and if the toolbar is found, we are using that, and if not found, we are creating a new bottom toolbar. Now let us define the saveChart function, which will be called by clicking on the **Download** button:

```
saveChart: function(){

  this.chart.save({
    type : 'image/png'
  });

}
```

Here we use the plugin within a window:

```
Ext.define('Examples.view.chartdownloadplugin.
ChartDownloadPluginWindow', {
  extend : 'Ext.Window',
  alias : 'widget.chartdownloadpluginwindow',
  requires : ['Examples.view.chartdownloadplugin.Chart',
              'Examples.plugin.ChartDownload'],

  constructor : function(config) {

    Ext.apply(this, {
      modal : true,
      width : 400,
      height : 300,
      title : 'ChartDownloadPlugin',
      layout : {
        type:'fit'
      },
      plugins:['chartdownload'],
        items : [Ext.create('Examples.view.chartdownloadplugin.
Chart')],
        buttons : [{
          text : 'OK',
          handler : function() {
```

```
            this.close();
        },
            scope : this
        }]
    });
    this.callParent(arguments);
  }
});
```

And the following screenshot is the output where we used our chart downloader plugin:

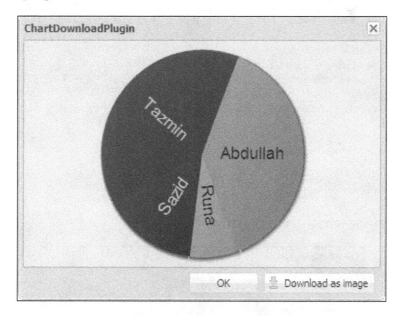

You can see that the **Download as image** button is generated at the window's bottom bar, and users can download the image by clicking on this button.

Now let us test this with another container that has no bottom bar defined:

```
Ext.define('Examples.view.chartdownloadplugin.
ChartDownloadPluginWindow', {
    extend : 'Ext.Window',
    alias : 'widget.chartdownloadpluginwindow',
    requires : ['Examples.view.chartdownloadplugin.Chart',
            'Examples.plugin.ChartDownload'],

    constructor : function(config) {
```

```
Ext.apply(this, {
  modal : true,
  width : 400,
  height : 300,
  title : 'ChartDownloadPlugin',
  layout : {
    type:'fit'
  },
  items : [{
    xtype:'panel',
    plugins:['chartdownload'],
    layout:'fit',
    items:[Ext.create('Examples.view.chartdownloadplugin.Chart')]
  }],
  buttons : [{
    text : 'OK',
    handler : function() {
      this.close();
    },
    scope : this
  }]
});
this.callParent(arguments);

  }
});
```

And the following screenshot is the output:

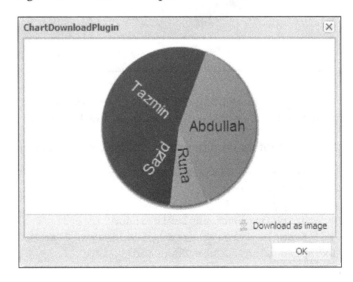

You can see that the download button is now generated within the nested panel's bottom bar.

Summary

In this chapter we've developed an Ext JS plugin that can download a chart as an image. Through this chapter we've learned the way we can create the Ext JS plugins and how easily we can inject functionality through the Ext JS plugins. In the next chapter, we will go through a very popular plugin for grid searching, where users can select or deselect the grid columns on which they want to apply the search.

6
Grid Search

In this chapter we are going to develop an Ext JS plugin, which will provide a search facility within a grid. This plugin was originally developed by Ing. Jozef Sakáloš and it is really useful and popular plugin. We will rewrite this plugin for the Ext JS 4x Version.

In this chapter we will cover:

- Functional requirements
- Planning and coding the grid search

Functional requirements

We want to develop a plugin, which will help users to search within a grid panel through a text field. The plugin will also offer users the option to select or deselect the columns of the grid on which they want to apply the searching. There will be a clear button to clear the search text. There will be a configuration option where users can set the number of characters they want in order to trigger the search by typing within the search textbox.

Planning and coding the grid search

To develop the plugin, we will create a menu where the user can select and deselect the columns of the grid, a text field where the user can write their search query, and a clear button that will help to clear the search query. At first we will develop the required UI fields and then we will add the corresponding functionality to those fields. Now let us start coding:

```
Ext.define("Examples.plugin.GridSearch", {

    extend : 'Ext.util.Observable',
    alias : 'plugin.gridsearch',

    config : {

        iconCls : 'icon-zoom',
        checkIndexes : "all",
        mode : 'local',
        minChars : 1,
        width : 100,
        searchText : 'Search',
        selectAllText : 'Select all',
        position: 'bottom' ,
        paramNames: {
            fields:'fields'
            ,query:'query'
        }

    },

    init : function(cmp) {

        this.grid = cmp.view.up('gridpanel');

        if (this.grid.rendered)
            this.onRender();
        else {
            this.grid.on('render', this.onRender, this);
        }

    },
    ...
```

You can see that we have defined several configuration options and also the required init function for the plugin. Now let us define the onRender function:

```
onRender : function() {

  var tb = this.getToolbar();
  this.menu = new Ext.menu.Menu();

  this.field = Ext.create("Ext.form.field.Trigger", {
    width : this.width,
    selectOnFocus : undefined === this.selectOnFocus ?
              true : this.selectOnFocus,
       triggerCls : 'x-form-clear-trigger',
       minLength : this.minLength
  });

  tb.add('->', {
    text : this.searchText,
    menu : this.menu,
    iconCls : this.iconCls
  }, this.field);


}
```

In this function, first we are trying to get the toolbar by calling the getToolbar function as we need to render our plugin UI on the toolbar. Then we are creating the menu field, which will hold the column selections, and then the search field. After this, we will add the menu field and the search field to that toolbar. Now let us define the getToolbar function:

```
getToolbar: function(){

  var me = this,
  dockedItems = this.grid.getDockedItems(),
  toolbar = null,
  hasToolbar = false;

  if(dockedItems.length>0){
    Ext.each(dockedItems, function(item){
      if(item.xtype ==='toolbar' && item.dock == me.position){
        hasToolbar = true;
        toolbar = item;
        return false;
      }
    });
```

```
  }

  if(!hasToolbar){
    toolbar = this.grid.addDocked({
      xtype: 'toolbar',
      dock: this.position
    })[0];
  }

  return toolbar;

}
```

In this function we are looking for a toolbar item, which is docked at the location defined in the position configuration option. We will render our plugin UI on this returned toolbar.

Now let us use this plugin within a grid and the output of the plugin should look like the following screenshot:

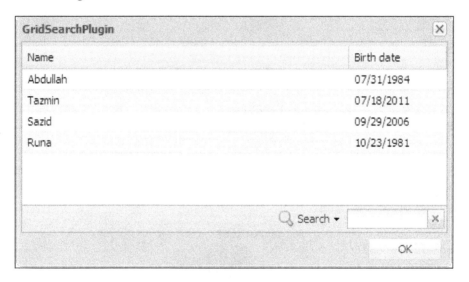

So, now we have our plugin looking exactly the same as the requirement. Now let us start adding functionality. First let us modify the onRender function of our plugin code:

```
this.field = Ext.create("Ext.form.field.Trigger", {
  width : this.width,
  selectOnFocus : undefined === this.selectOnFocus ?
            true : this.selectOnFocus,
     triggerCls : 'x-form-clear-trigger',
  onTriggerClick : Ext.bind(this.onTriggerClear, this),
       minLength : this.minLength
});
```

You can see that we have provided the onTriggerClear handler for the onTriggerClick event to clear the search. We need to add and handle some keyboard events: pressing the *Enter* key will trigger searching and pressing the *Esc* key will trigger clearing the search. So, we need to add the following code after defining the trigger field:

```
this.field.on('render', function() {

  if (this.minChars) {
    this.field.el.on({
      scope : this,
      buffer : 300,
      keyup : this.onKeyUp
    });
  }

  var map = new Ext.KeyMap(this.field.el, [{
    key : Ext.EventObject.ENTER,
    scope : this,
    fn : this.onTriggerSearch
  }, {
    key : Ext.EventObject.ESC,
    scope : this,
    fn : this.onTriggerClear
  }]);
  map.stopEvent = true;
}, this, {
  single : true
});
```

Now, we need to prepare the menu to load the column names and we will call the `initMenu` function to do that. And that's all we needed to do within the `onRender` function.

Now let us define the `onKeyUp` handler:

```
onKeyUp : function(e) {

  if (e.isNavKeyPress()) {
    return;
  }

  var length = this.field.getValue().toString().length;
  if (0 === length || this.minChars <= length) {
    this.onTriggerSearch();
  }

}
```

Let us go ahead with defining the `initMenu` function:

```
initMenu : function() {

  var menu = this.menu;
  menu.removeAll();

  menu.add(new Ext.menu.CheckItem({
    text : this.selectAllText,
    checked : !(this.checkIndexes instanceof Array),
    hideOnClick : false,
    handler : function(item) {
      var checked = item.checked;
      menu.items.each(function(i) {
        if (item !== i && i.setChecked && !i.disabled) {
          i.setChecked(checked);
        }
      });
    }
  }), '-');

  var cm = this.grid.headerCt.items.items;

  var group = undefined;
  Ext.each(cm, function(item) {
    var config = item.initialConfig;
```

```
        var disable = false;

        if (config.header && config.dataIndex) {
          Ext.each(this.disableIndexes, function(item) {
            disable = disable ? disable :
              item === config.dataIndex;
          });
          if (!disable) {
            menu.add(new Ext.menu.CheckItem({
              text : config.header,
              hideOnClick : false,
              group : group,
              checked : 'all' === this.checkIndexes,
              dataIndex : config.dataIndex
            }));
          }
        }
      }, this);

      if (this.checkIndexes instanceof Array) {
        Ext.each(this.checkIndexes, function(di) {
          var item = menu.items.find(function(itm) {
            return itm.dataIndex === di;
          });
          if (item) {
            item.setChecked(true, true);
          }
        }, this);
      }


    }
```

You can see how we are preparing the menu for selecting and deselecting the
columns in the preceding `initMenu` function. Now let us define the `onTriggerClear`
function, which is responsible for clearing the search query:

```
onTriggerClear : function() {

  if (this.field.getValue()) {
    this.field.reset();
    this.field.focus();
    this.onTriggerSearch();
  }

}
```

Next we define the `onTriggerSearch` function:

```
onTriggerSearch : function() {

  if (!this.field.isValid()) {
    return;
  }
  var val = this.field.getValue(),
    store = this.grid.store,
    proxy = store.getProxy();
  ...
```

We need to check against the value set for the `mode` configuration option and need to provide separate logic if the value is set to `'local'` or if the proxy of the store is a server proxy. Now we need to add the following code within the `onTriggerSearch` function when the mode is set with `'local'`:

```
if ('local' === this.mode) {
  store.clearFilter();
  if (val) {
    store.filterBy(function(r) {
      var retval = false;
      this.menu.items.each(function(item) {
        if (!item.dataIndex || !item.checked || retval) {
          return;
        }

        var rv = r.get(item.dataIndex), rv = rv instanceof Date ?
        Ext.Date.format(rv, this.getDateFormat(item)) : rv;
        var re = new RegExp(Ext.String.escape(val), 'gi');
        retval = re.test(rv);
      }, this);
      if (retval) {
        return true;
      }
      return retval;
    }, this);
  }
}
```

And if the value is not set to `local`, we need to check whether the proxy is a server proxy or not. And here is the code that we need to add within the `onTriggerSearch` function after the `if ('local' === this.mode)` block:

```
else if(proxy instanceof Ext.data.proxy.Server) {

    if(store.lastOptions && store.lastOptions.params) {
        store.lastOptions.params[store.paramNames.start] = 0;
    }

    var fields = [];
    this.menu.items.each(function(item) {
        if(item.checked && item.dataIndex) {
            fields.push(item.dataIndex);
        }
    });

    delete(proxy.extraParams[this.paramNames.fields]);
    delete(proxy.extraParams[this.paramNames.query]);
    if (store.lastOptions && store.lastOptions.params) {
        delete(proxy.lastOptions.params[this.paramNames.fields]);
        delete(proxy.lastOptions.params[this.paramNames.query]);
    }
    if(fields.length) {
        proxy.extraParams[this.paramNames.fields] = Ext.encode(fields);
        proxy.extraParams[this.paramNames.query] = val;
    }

    store.load();
}
```

Now we define the `getDateFormat` function:

```
getDateFormat : function(menuItem) {

    var columnNames = Ext.Array.pluck(this.grid.columns, 'dataIndex'),
    columnIndex = Ext.Array.indexOf(columnNames, menuItem.dataIndex),
    format = this.grid.columns[columnIndex].format;

    return this.dateFormat || format;
}
```

Following is the screenshot of our working plugin:

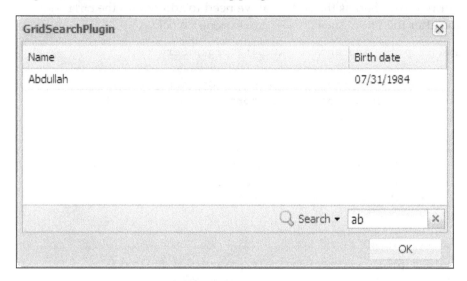

You can see that our plugin filters data according to the search query.

Summary

In this chapter we've developed an Ext JS plugin to provide searching facility within a grid. Now we have a clear idea about how powerful the Ext JS plugins are. We can easily use this plugin within a grid and can provide this excellent searching feature whenever we need.

In the next chapter we will go through another useful plugin targeted for text components that show a clear button over the text field, and we will see how clicking on the button will clear the texts from the text field.

7
Input Field with Clear Button

In this chapter we will go through Stephen Friedrich's `ClearButton` plugin. This plugin is targeted for text components that show a "clear" button over the text field. When the clear button is clicked on, the text field is emptied. Also, the icon image and its positioning can be controlled using CSS.

The topics covered are:

- Functional requirements
- Planning and coding of the clear button

Functional requirements

We want a plugin that will help users to clear the text within the text components, such as `Ext.form.field.Text`, `Ext.form.field.TextArea`, `Ext.form.field.ComboBox`, and `Ext.form.field.Date`. The plugin should provide a button to click on in order to clear the text within a text component. This plugin should have several useful configuration options and CSS styles, where we can set our requirements, such as the clear button should always/only show up when the mouse enters within the input field, or it should be shown when the input field is empty or is cleared when the user presses *Esc*. The clear button can be customized for button image/position via CSS, and so on.

Planning and coding of the clear button

To develop this plugin we will first create the clear button that will be rendered over the text component, and will apply the CSS styles according to the configuration options. After that, we need to add several event handlers for the clear button, such as `click`, `mouseover`, `mouseout`, `mouseup`, and `mousedown`, and also, several event handlers for the text component, such as `destroy`, `resize`, `change`, `mouseover`, and `mouseout`. Let us now start coding:

```
Ext.define('Examples.plugin.ClearButton', {
  alias : 'plugin.clearbutton',

  hideClearButtonWhenEmpty : true,
  hideClearButtonWhenMouseOut : true,
  animateClearButton : true,
  clearOnEscape : true,
  clearButtonCls : 'ext-ux-clearbutton',
  textField : null,
  animateWithCss3 : false,

  constructor : function(cfg) {
    Ext.apply(this, cfg);

    this.callParent(arguments);
  },

  init : function(textField) {
    this.textField = textField;
    if (!textField.rendered) {
      textField.on('afterrender', this.handleAfterRender, this);
    }
    else {
      this.handleAfterRender();
    }
  }
}
```

In the preceding code snippet, you can see that we have defined several configuration options, and the required `init` function.

Now let us define the `handleAfterRender` function:

```
handleAfterRender : function(textField) {
  this.isTextArea = (this.textField.inputEl.dom.type.
    toLowerCase() == 'textarea');
  this.createClearButtonEl();
  this.addListeners();
  this.repositionClearButton();
  this.updateClearButtonVisibility();
  this.addEscListener();
}
```

Within this `handleAfterRender` function, at first, we are checking whether the textfield is a `textarea` or not, as we need to handle `textarea` with custom functionality since this field may have a scrollbar. And then we call the `createClearButtonEl` function to create the element and the DOM for the clear button.

Now let us define the `createClearButtonEl` function:

```
createClearButtonEl : function() {
  var animateWithClass = this.animateClearButton &&
    this.animateWithCss3;
  this.clearButtonEl = this.textField.bodyEl.createChild({
    tag : 'div',
    cls : this.clearButtonCls
  });
  if (this.animateClearButton) {
    this.animateWithCss3 = this.supportsCssTransition(
      this.clearButtonEl);
  }
  if (this.animateWithCss3) {
    this.clearButtonEl.addCls(this.clearButtonCls + '-off');
  }
  else {
    this.clearButtonEl.setStyle('visibility', 'hidden');
  }
}
```

In the preceding function the clear button has been created and assigned an animation, based on the configuration options. In this function we also checked whether the browser supports CSS3 transitions or not, by calling the supportsCssTransition function.

Now, let us define the supportsCssTransition function:

```
supportsCssTransition: function(el) {
  var styles = ['transitionProperty', 'WebkitTransitionProperty',
    'MozTransitionProperty', 'OTransitionProperty',
      'msTransitionProperty', 'KhtmlTransitionProperty'];

  var style = el.dom.style;
  for(var i = 0, length = styles.length; i < length; ++i) {
    if(style[styles[i]] !== 'undefined') {
      return true;
    }
  }
  return false;
}
```

The next function we are calling within the handleAfterRender function is the addListeners function to add listeners to the field, its input element, and the clear button to handle resizing events such as mouseover, mouseout, and click.

Now, let us define the addListeners function:

```
addListeners: function() {
  var textField = this.textField;
  var bodyEl = textField.bodyEl;
  bodyEl.on('mouseover', this.handleMouseOverInputField, this);
  bodyEl.on('mouseout', this.handleMouseOutOfInputField, this);

  textField.on('destroy', this.handleDestroy, this);
  textField.on('resize', this.repositionClearButton, this);
  textField.on('change', function() {
    this.repositionClearButton();
    this.updateClearButtonVisibility();
  }, this);

  var clearButtonEl = this.clearButtonEl;
  clearButtonEl.on('mouseover', this.handleMouseOverClearButton,
    this);
  clearButtonEl.on('mouseout', this.handleMouseOutOfClearButton,
    this);
```

```
    clearButtonEl.on('mousedown', this.handleMouseDownOnClearButton,
      this);
    clearButtonEl.on('mouseup', this.handleMouseUpOnClearButton,
      this);
  clearButtonEl.on('click', this.handleMouseClickOnClearButton,
    this);
}
```

Next we define the mouseover event handler – handleMouseOverInputField, and the mouseout event handler – handleMouseOutOfInputField, for bodyEl of textField:

```
handleMouseOverInputField: function(event, htmlElement, object) {
  this.clearButtonEl.addCls(this.clearButtonCls +
    '-mouse-over-input');
  if (event.getRelatedTarget() == this.clearButtonEl.dom) {
    this.clearButtonEl.removeCls(this.clearButtonCls +
      '-mouse-over-button');
    this.clearButtonEl.removeCls(this.clearButtonCls +
      '-mouse-down');
  }
  this.updateClearButtonVisibility();
},
handleMouseOutOfInputField: function(event, htmlElement, object) {
  this.clearButtonEl.removeCls(this.clearButtonCls +
    '-mouse-over-input');
  if (event.getRelatedTarget() == this.clearButtonEl.dom) {
    this.clearButtonEl.addCls(this.clearButtonCls +
      '-mouse-over-button');
  }
  this.updateClearButtonVisibility();
}
```

Now let us define the "destroy" event handler of textField since when the field is destroyed, we also need to destroy the clear button element to prevent memory leaks:

```
handleDestroy: function() {
  this.clearButtonEl.destroy();
}
```

Now let us start defining the handlers for the clear button's mouseover, mouseout, mousedown, mouseup, and click events:

```
handleMouseOverClearButton: function(event, htmlElement, object) {
  event.stopEvent();
  if (this.textField.bodyEl.contains(event.getRelatedTarget())) {
    return;
  }
  this.clearButtonEl.addCls(this.clearButtonCls +
    '-mouse-over-button');
  this.updateClearButtonVisibility();
},

handleMouseOutOfClearButton: function(event, htmlElement, object){
  event.stopEvent();
  if (this.textField.bodyEl.contains(event.getRelatedTarget())) {
    return;
  }
  this.clearButtonEl.removeCls(this.clearButtonCls +
    '-mouse-over-button');
    this.clearButtonEl.removeCls(this.clearButtonCls +
    '-mouse-down');
  this.updateClearButtonVisibility();
},

handleMouseDownOnClearButton: function(event, htmlElement,
  object){
  if (!this.isLeftButton(event)) {
    return;
  }
  this.clearButtonEl.addCls(this.clearButtonCls +
    '-mouse-down');
},

handleMouseUpOnClearButton: function(event, htmlElement, object) {
  if (!this.isLeftButton(event)) {
    return;
  }
  this.clearButtonEl.removeCls(this.clearButtonCls +
    '-mouse-down');
},

handleMouseClickOnClearButton: function(event, htmlElement, object) {
  if (!this.isLeftButton(event)) {
    return;
  }
  this.textField.setValue('');
  this.textField.focus();
}
```

The next function we will call within the `handleAfterRender` function is the `repositionClearButton` function, to reposition the clear button element based on the `inputEl` element of `textField`. Now, let us define this function:

```
repositionClearButton: function() {
  var clearButtonEl = this.clearButtonEl;
  if (!clearButtonEl) {
    return;
  }
  var clearButtonPosition = this.calculateClearButtonPosition(
    this.textField);
  clearButtonEl.dom.style.right = clearButtonPosition.right +
    'px';
  clearButtonEl.dom.style.top = clearButtonPosition.top + 'px';
}
```

You can see that we get the clear button's position value by calling the `calculateClearButtonPosition` function. This function calculates the position of the clear button, based on the `inputEl` element of `textField`. Now, let us define this function:

```
calculateClearButtonPosition: function(textField) {
  var positions = textField.inputEl.getBox(true, true);
  var top = positions.y;
  var right = positions.x;
  if (this.fieldHasScrollBar()) {
    right += Ext.getScrollBarWidth();
  }
  if (this.textField.triggerWrap) {
    right += this.textField.getTriggerWidth();
  }
  return {
    right: right,
    top: top
  };
}
```

You can see that we checked whether the field has a scrollbar or not, and if the field has a scrollbar, we add the value of the `Ext.getScrollBarWidth` function to the `right` position. Now, let us define the `fieldHasScrollBar` function:

```
fieldHasScrollBar: function() {
  if (!this.isTextArea) {
    return false;
  }

  var inputEl = this.textField.inputEl;
  var overflowY = inputEl.getStyle('overflow-y');
  if (overflowY == 'hidden' || overflowY == 'visible') {
    return false;
  }
  if (overflowY == 'scroll') {
    return true;
  }
  if (inputEl.dom.scrollHeight <= inputEl.dom.clientHeight) {
    return false;
  }
  return true;
}
```

And then we called the `updateClearButtonVisibility` function within the `handleAfterRender` function for fixing the clear button's visibility:

```
updateClearButtonVisibility: function() {
  var oldVisible = this.isButtonCurrentlyVisible();
  var newVisible = this.shouldButtonBeVisible();

  var clearButtonEl = this.clearButtonEl;
  if (oldVisible != newVisible) {
    if(this.animateClearButton && this.animateWithCss3) {
      this.clearButtonEl.removeCls(this.clearButtonCls +
        (oldVisible ? '-on' : '-off'));
      clearButtonEl.addCls(this.clearButtonCls + (
        newVisible ? '-on' : '-off'));
    }
    else {
      clearButtonEl.stopAnimation();
      clearButtonEl.setVisible(newVisible,
        this.animateClearButton);
    }
```

```
clearButtonEl.setStyle('background-color',
    this.textField.inputEl.getStyle('background-color'));

if (!(this.isTextArea && Ext.isGecko) && !Ext.isIE) {
    var deltaPaddingRight = clearButtonEl.getWidth() - this.
        clearButtonEl.getMargin('l');
    var currentPaddingRight = this.textField.inputEl.
        getPadding('r');
    var factor = (newVisible ? +1 : -1);
    this.textField.inputEl.dom.style.paddingRight = (
        currentPaddingRight + factor * deltaPaddingRight) + 'px';
    }
  }
}
```

You can see that we took the value of the current visible state, and what will
be the new visible state, by calling the isButtonCurrentlyVisible and
shouldButtonBeVisible functions. The isButtonCurrentlyVisible function is a
wrapper around clearButtonEl.isVisible() to handle the setVisible animation
that may still be in progress, and the shouldButtonBeVisible function checks the
configuration options and the current mouse status to determine whether the clear
button should be visible or not. Now, let us define these functions:

```
isButtonCurrentlyVisible: function() {
    if (this.animateClearButton && this.animateWithCss3) {
        return this.clearButtonEl.hasCls(this.clearButtonCls + '-on');
    }
    var cachedVisible = Ext.core.Element.data(
        this.clearButtonEl.dom, 'isVisible');
    if (typeof(cachedVisible) == 'boolean') {
        return cachedVisible;
    }
    return this.clearButtonEl.isVisible();
},

shouldButtonBeVisible: function() {
    if (this.hideClearButtonWhenEmpty && Ext.isEmpty(
        this.textField.getValue())) {

        return false;
    }

    var clearButtonEl = this.clearButtonEl;
```

```
    if (this.hideClearButtonWhenMouseOut && !clearButtonEl.hasCls(
      this.clearButtonCls + '-mouse-over-button') && !clearButtonEl.
        hasCls(this.clearButtonCls + '-mouse-over-input')) {

      return false;
    }

    return true;
}
```

And the last function that we called within the `handleAfterRender` function is the `addEscListener` function. What we need to do is, if the configuration option `clearOnEscape` is set to `true`, add a key listener that will clear this field. Now, let us define this function:

```
addEscListener: function() {
  if (!this.clearOnEscape) {
    return;
  }

  this.textField.inputEl.on('keydown', function(e) {
    if (e.getKey() == Ext.EventObject.ESC) {
      if (this.textField.isExpanded) {
        return;
      }
      Ext.Function.defer(this.textField.setValue, 1,
        this.textField, ['']);
      e.stopEvent();
    }
  },
  this);
}
```

The following screenshot is the output where we've used this plugin for **textfield, textareafield, combobox,** and the date field:

You can see that on hovering over the **textfield** component, the clear button is visible and clicking on this button will clear the respective field.

Summary

In this chapter we've gone through an Ext JS plugin, which provides a clear button for text components to clear the content within it. We can see that developing a single plugin can be used in several types of components, and how easily we can inject the functionality of the plugin.

In the next chapter we will develop an Ext JS extension for a fancy animated message bar. The message bar will provide a facility to have a configurable duration timer for showing a message. It will have a close button, and it will also be able to show an "error" and a "successful" icon, beside the message.

8
Message Bar

In this chapter, we are going to develop an Ext JS extension, which will be a fancy animated message bar. The message bar will provide the facility for having a configurable duration timer for showing the message, a close button, and also will be able to customize the look and can provide optional icons for different types of states such as valid, invalid, or information during runtime.

In this chapter, we will cover:

- Functional requirements
- Planning and coding the message bar

Functional requirements

We are targeting to develop an Ext JS extension that can be used to show messages. This extension can be used within a container as a docked item to show messages. The message bar will be closed automatically when the configured timer is completed. This message bar will also provide a close button and on clicking on this button the message bar will be closed. The opening and closing of the message bar will be in a smooth animated form. This message bar can also accept configuration at runtime to show several types of state that it can change its look to, and can show a proper icon.

Planning and coding the message bar

To develop this extension, we can use the Ext JS toolbar and dock it to the bottom of the container. Then we can add a functionality where this toolbar can show the message text. Then we need to add a functionality when the message bar is called to show the message; the message bar appears and disappears when the close button is clicked upon or when the configured timer is completed. As per our functional requirement, we can see that the Ext JS library provided StatusBar extension is doing a lot that we needed to provide functionality for this message bar extension. So, we can modify that extension and add our own functionality and CSS styles to fulfill our requirement. Now let us start coding:

```
Ext.define('Examples.ux.MessageBar', {
  extend: 'Ext.toolbar.Toolbar',
  alias: 'widget.ux-msgbar',
  activeThreadId: 0,
  dock: 'bottom',
  config: {
    cls: 'x-messagebar',
    emptyText: '',
    defaultText: '',
    autoClear: 5000
  },


  initComponent: function () {
    this.callParent(arguments);
  },
  ...
```

After defining the class configuration, now let us create the element where the message text will be shown—the icon and the close button. Now let us define the afterRender handler where we will create those elements:

```
afterRender: function () {

  this.el.addCls('x-message-msgbar-body');

  this.currIconCls = this.iconCls || this.defaultIconCls;
  var me = this;

  setTimeout(function () {

    var tpl = new Ext.XTemplate(
      '<div id="{id}-bar" class="{bodyCls}"',
```

```
      ' style="width: {width}px; {left}">',
      '<div class="{msgCls}"></div>',
      '<div style="float:right" class="{closeCls}">X</div>',
      '</div>'
    );

    tpl = tpl.apply({
      id: me.id,
      bodyCls: 'x-message-msgbar-body',
      width: me.ownerCt.getWidth() - 10,
      left: Ext.isIE8 ? 'left:5px' : '',
      msgCls: 'x-message-bar-msg',
      closeCls: 'x-message-bar-close'
    });

    me.ownerCt.el.createChild(tpl);

    Ext.select('.x-message-bar-close').on('click', function () {
      me.clearMessage();
    });

  }, 500);

  this.hide();
  this.callParent(arguments);
}
```

You can see how we are creating those elements. We have also defined the click handler for the close button. We are calling the `clearMessage` function whenever the close button is clicked. We will define this function later in this chapter.
We need to take care that whenever the container is resized, we also need to resize the message bar element. So, now let us add some code to handle this within the `afterRender` handler:

```
this.ownerCt.on('resize', function (ownerContainer, width, height) {
  if (width == this.parentWidth && height == this.parentHeight) {
    return;
  }

  var bar = Ext.get(this.id + '-bar');

  if (bar) {
    bar.setStyle('width', (this.ownerCt.getWidth()-10)  + 'px');
  }
}, this);
```

Now let us define the showMessage function, which will be called to show the message with the provided configuration:

```
showMessage: function (msg) {

  if (Ext.isString(msg)) {
    msg = {
      text: msg
    }
  }

  this.setMessage({
    text: msg.text,
    iconCls: 'x-message-'
    + (msg.type || '') + ' ',
    clear: Ext.isDefined(msg.clear) ? msg.clear : true
  });

}
```

Within this function, we are checking the provided configuration and preparing the configuration properly and sending that to the setMessage function. Now let us define the setMessage function:

```
setMessage: function (o) {
  if (o && (o.text == '' || o.text == ' ')) {
    return;
  } else {
    var cmp = Ext.get(this.id + '-bar');
    if (cmp) {
      cmp.slideIn('b', {
        duration: 300,
        easing: 'easeIn',
        callback: function () {
          this.setMessageData(o);
        },
        scope: this
      });
    }
  }
}
```

In this function, we are checking whether the message text is empty or not, and if it is not empty, we are opening the message bar and calling the `setMessageData` function to set the message text, UI, and proper icon for the message bar. Let us now define the `setMessageData` function:

```
setMessageData: function (o) {
  o = o || {};
  if (o.text !== undefined) {
    this.setText(o.text);
  }
  if (o.iconCls !== undefined) {
    var bar = Ext.get(this.id + '-bar');
    if (o.iconCls == 'x-message-error ') {
      bar.removeCls('x-message-msg-body');
      bar.addCls('x-message-error-body');
    } else {
      bar.removeCls('x-message-error-body');
      bar.addCls('x-message-msg-body');
    }
    this.setIcon(o.iconCls);
  }
  if (o.clear) {
    var c = o.clear, wait = this.autoClear, defaults = {
      useDefaults: true,
      anim: true
    };
    if (Ext.isObject(c)) {
      c = Ext.applyIf(c, defaults);
      if (c.wait) {
        wait = c.wait;
      }
    } else if (Ext.isNumber(c)) {
      wait = c;
      c = defaults;
    } else if (Ext.isBoolean(c)) {
      c = defaults;
    }
    c.threadId = this.activeThreadId;
    if (this.clearTimer) {
      clearTimeout(this.clearTimer);
    }
    this.clearTimer = Ext.defer(this.clearMessage, wait, this, [c]);
  }
}
```

You can see that within this function we are setting the message text, icon, and UI. To set the message text we are calling the setText function, to change the UI we are adding and removing the corresponding CSS classes, and to set the icon we are calling the setIcon function. Also, when the clear configuration option is set to true, we are applying the configured timer to hide the message bar when the timer is completed. Now let us define the clearMessage function:

```
clearMessage: function (o) {
  o = o || {};
  if (o.threadId && o.threadId !== this.activeThreadId) {
    return this;
  }
  var bar = Ext.get(this.id + '-bar');
  if (bar) {
    Ext.get(this.id + '-bar').slideOut('b', {
      duration: 300,
      easing: 'easeOut',
      callback: function () {
        var text = o.useDefaults ? this.defaultText : this.emptyText,
        iconCls = o.useDefaults ? (this.defaultIconCls ? this.
defaultIconCls : '') : '';
        this.setMessage({
          text: text,
          iconCls: iconCls
        });
      },
      scope: this
    });
  }
  return this;
}
```

And here in this clearMessage function we are hiding the message bar.

Now let us have some test with this extension. Here in the following screenshot you can see our message bar extension in action. We have created an Ext JS window and added the message bar as a docked item.

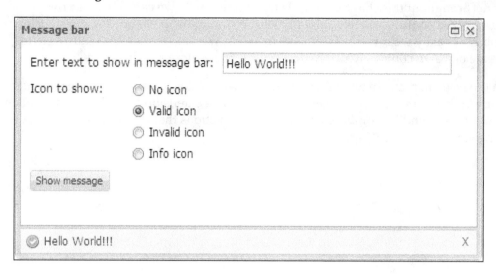

You can see that the message bar appears with the configured data when you click on the **Show message** button. And when we choose the **Invalid icon** option, we can see how the message bar changes its look. Here you can see the result when we choose the **Invalid icon**:

From the preceding screenshots we can see that our extension is working exactly the way we wanted.

Summary

In this chapter, we've developed an Ext JS extension, a fancy animated message bar. Throughout this chapter we've learned how easily we can create our own customized control. As we've already learned about the power of Ext JS extension and how easily we can create Ext JS extensions, we can see that it is really easy to create our own control, which helps to fulfill our custom requirements.

In the next chapter, we will go through another Ext JS extension BoxSelect, which was originally developed by Kevin Vaughan. This extension is really very useful and provides a friendlier combobox for multiple selections that create removable labels for each selection easily and individually.

Intuitive Multiselect Combobox

9

In this chapter we will explore an excellent Ext JS extension: `BoxSelect`, which was originally developed by Kevin Vaughan. This extension is really very useful and provides a friendlier combobox for multiple selections that creates removable labels for each selection, easily and individually, and lots more.

The topics covered are:

- Features of `BoxSelect`
- The `BoxSelect` extension:
  - Basic configuration
  - Templates
  - Single value selection
  - Remote query with unknown values
  - Adding new records with autosuggestion
  - `BoxSelect` specific configurations
  - Value handling and events

Features of BoxSelect

BoxSelect is an extended ComboBox component developed for more intuitive multiselect capabilities. BoxSelect comes with lots of examples and proper documentation. The following features are provided by the BoxSelect extension:

- Selected items can be removed individually.
- Customizable item templates for controlling the display of the selected values.
- Supports keyboard-based selection and navigation for the selected values.
- Supports on-demand loading of values from remote stores when an unknown value is set, and the queryMode option is set to remote and forceSelection is set to true.
- Setting forceSelection to false creates new records.
- When multiSelect is set to true the pick list can be configured to tell if it should collapse or not, after making a selection.
- Selected items can be configured to be stacked or autosized.
- Most of the existing functionalities and configuration options of ComboBox should work with BoxSelect.

Using BoxSelect

BoxSelect extends the ComboBox control to provide a more multiselect, friendly ComboBox control. The examples included in this chapter show the differences between the default ComboBox control and this extension, and provide general information about the advanced usage of BoxSelect.

Basic configuration

BoxSelect should support all configuration values as the ComboBox supports. There are some changes for the default values for this extension:

- The multiSelect option is set to true by default.
- The forceSelection option is set to true by default.
- In most cases, the multiple selections are made from a preformed list, but we can also configure the BoxSelect extension to add new records with an autosuggestion list.

- The ComboBox component doesn't support typeAhead when the multiSelect option is set to true, but even though the value of typeAhead is set to false by default for the BoxSelect extension, support for this feature has been added for multiSelect when set to true.

- The value option can be used to initialize the multiSelect values. The same format of values is accepted for the setValue method.

Now, let us start using the BoxSelect extension with the following configuration:

```
{
    "value": [
        "TX",
        "CA"
    ],
    "fieldLabel": "Select multiple states",
    "displayField": "name",
    "valueField": "abbr",
    "width": 500,
    "labelWidth": 130,
    "emptyText": "Pick a state, any state",
    "store": "States",
    "queryMode": "local"
}
```

And the screenshot should be as follows:

In the preceding screenshot, we can see how easily we can select multiple values within the BoxSelect combobox extension.

Templates

We can easily configure the display of the selected values and the drop-down list items through templates:

- **labelTpl**: It is the template configuration option which controls the display of the selected values within the input field.

- **listConfig**: It is the template configuration option which controls the display of the drop-down list items. This option is available within the default ComboBox field and also supported by BoxSelect.

Now, let us see how we can set the configuration for customizing the `labelTpl` and the `listConfig` options:

```
{
    "delimiter": ", ",
    "value": "AZ, CA, NC",
    "labelTpl": "<img src=\"{flagUrl}\"
                      style=\"height: 25px;
                      vertical-align: middle;
                      margin: 2px;\" /> {name} ({abbr})",
    "listConfig": {
      "tpl": [
        "<ul><tpl for=\".\">",
        "<li role=\"option\"
              class=\"x-boundlist-item\"
              style=\"background-image:url({flagUrl});
              background-repeat: no-repeat;
              background-size: 25px;
              padding-left: 30px;\">{name}: {slogan}</li>",
          "</tpl></ul>"
      ]
    },
    "fieldLabel": "Select multiple states",
    "displayField": "name",
    "valueField": "abbr",
    "width": 500,
    "labelWidth": 130,

    "store": "States",
    "queryMode": "local"
}
```

Following is the screenshot of the `BoxSelect` extension using the preceding configuration for `labelTpl` and `listConfig`:

In the preceding screenshot, we can see that the BoxSelect extension is working fine and is showing the selected items with the configured labelTpl and listConfig comboboxes.

Single value selection

The BoxSelect extension is targeted for multiple selections, but it also supports single selection by setting the multiSelect option to false. If we need the single selection option by default, we can add the following line of code before the BoxSelect extension is created:

```
Ext.ux.form.field.BoxSelect.prototype.multiSelect = false;
```

Now, let us configure the BoxSelect extension for a single selection:

```
{
    "fieldLabel": "Select a state",
    "multiSelect": false,
    "filterPickList": true,
    "displayField": "name",
    "valueField": "abbr",
    "width": 500,
    "labelWidth": 130,
    "emptyText": "Pick a state, any state",
    "store": "States",
    "queryMode": "local"
}
```

And the output should be as follows:

In the preceding screenshot, we can now select only a single value within the combobox when the multiSelect option is set to false.

Remote query with unknown values

When we set the `queryMode` option to `remote` and the `forceSelection` option to `true`, and we pass a value to the `BoxSelect` extension that is not in the store, a query will be sent to the store's configured proxy "x" with the name of the `valueField` option and a set of unknown values separated by the configured `delimiter` as the parameters. For example, if the `valueField` option is `abbr`, the `delimiter` value is `|`, and unknown values 'NC', 'VA', and, 'ZZ' are set, the following parameters will be passed to the store's configured proxy:

```
{ abbr: 'NC|VA|ZZ' }
```

This attempt to load the unknown values will be performed only once per `initValue`/`setValue` call. The records which are still unknown after this request will be removed from the field's value, but all known values will be retained. In the preceding example, the 'ZZ' entry was discarded.

Now, let us configure the `BoxSelect` extension for remote stores:

```
{
  "fieldLabel": "With Remote Store",
  "store": "RemoteStates",
  "pageSize": 25,
  "queryMode": "remote",
  "delimiter": "|",
  "value": "NC|VA|ZZ",
  "triggerOnClick": false,
  "labelTpl": "{name} ({abbr})",
  "listConfig": {
    "tpl": [
      "<ul><tpl for=\".\">",
        "<li role=\"option\"
              class=\"x-boundlist-item\">{name}: {slogan}</li>",
      "</tpl></ul>"
    ]
  },
  "displayField": "name",
  "valueField": "abbr",
  "width": 500,
  "labelWidth": 130
}
```

Following is the screenshot where we have used this configuration for the `BoxSelect` extension:

In the preceding screenshot we can see that our configured `BoxSelect` is working fine for the remote store, and the value for 'NC' and 'VA' is retrieved where the value for 'ZZ' is discarded.

Adding new records with autosuggestion

In this example we will show the use of `forceSelection`, when set to `false`, to enable the entry of new values with autosuggestion provided from the attached store. The new records will be created using the user input for both the configured `displayField` and `valueField`. These new records are not added to the `ComboBox` store automatically.

New entries can be created by any of the following four ways:

- When we type the configured `delimiter` which is default to ',', the value that we entered before the `delimiter` will be used to create a new record.

- When we paste texts in to the field, the value will be split according to the configured `delimiter`, which is default to ',' and any values entered will be parsed in to new/existing records.

- The `createNewOnEnter` option is set to `false` by default. If set to `true`, a new entry will be created when we press the *Enter* key. This configuration option only applies if the `forceSelection` option is set to `false`.

- The `createNewOnBlur` option is set to `false` by default. If set to `true`, a new entry will be created when the focus leaves the input field. This configuration option only applies if `forceSelection` is set to `false`, and is superseded by `autoSelect` and `selectOnTab`.

Now, let us configure the `BoxSelect` extension for autosuggestion:

```
{
  "fieldLabel": "Enter multiple email addresses",
  "width": 500,
  "growMin": 75,
  "growMax": 120,
  "labelWidth": 130,
  "store": [
    "test@example.com",
    "somebody@somewhere.net",
    "johnjacob@jingleheimerschmidts.org",
    "rumpelstiltskin@guessmyname.com",
    "fakeaddresses@arefake.com",
    "bob@thejoneses.com"
  ],
  "queryMode": "local",
  "forceSelection": false,
  "createNewOnEnter": true,
  "createNewOnBlur": true,
  "filterPickList": true,
  "displayField": "name",
  "valueField": "abbr"
}
```

Using this configuration we will get the `BoxSelect` component as follows:

In the preceding screenshot, we can see how the `BoxSelect` component is offering an autosuggestion list where we can select those list items or create new records.

BoxSelect specific configurations

The following configuration options are specific to the BoxSelect extension:

- The createNewOnEnter option is set to false by default. If this option is set to true and the forceSelection option is set to false, a new entry will be created as soon as the user presses the *Enter* key.

- The createNewOnBlur option is set to false by default. If this option is set to true and the forceSelection option is set to false, a new entry will be created when the focus leaves the input field. This configuration option is superseded by autoSelect and selectOnTab.

- The stacked option is set to false by default. If this option is set to true, the labeled items will fill the available width of the list instead of being only as wide as the displayed value.

- The pinList option is set to true by default. If this option is set to false, the pick list will automatically collapse after a selection is made, when multiSelect is true. This mimics the default behavior when multiSelect is false.

- The triggerOnClick option is set to true by default. When the option is set to true, the pick list will emulate a trigger when clicking in the field just like when a ComboBox component is set with the editable option to false.

- The grow option is set to true by default. If this option is set to false, the list of selections will scroll when necessary, and the height of the field will not change. This setting has no effect if a fixed height is set for the field, either directly (for example, through a height configuration), or by the containing layout.

- The growMin option is set to false by default. If this option is set to true, any numeric value will be used for the field's minimum height.

- The growMax option is set to false by default. If this option is set to true, any numeric value will be used for the field's maximum height and the list of selections will scroll when necessary.

- The filterPickList option is set to false by default. If this option is set to true, the currently selected values will be hidden from the expanded pick list.

Now, let us configure the `BoxSelect` component by changing some of the default values to see the effect:

```
{
    "fieldLabel": "Select multiple states",
    "displayField": "name",
    "width": 500,
    "labelWidth": 130,
    "store": "States",
    "queryMode": "local",
    "valueField": "abbr",
    "value": "WA, TX",
    "stacked": true,
    "pinList": false,
    "filterPickList": true
}
```

Following is the screenshot of the `BoxSelect` component where we've used this configuration:

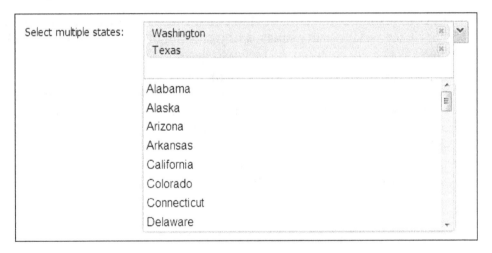

In the preceding screenshot, we can see that the labeled items are filling the full width available as we set the `stacked` option to `true`. The pick list is automatically collapsing as soon as a selection is made as we set the `pinList` option to `false`, and the current selected values are hidden from the expanded pick list as we set the `filterPickList` option to `true`.

Value handling and events

The following methods are available within `BoxSelect`, which helps to work with the value of the combobox:

- `addValue(mixedValue)`: Adds a value or values to the current value of the field.

- `removeValue(mixedValue)`: Removes a value or values from the current value of the field.

- `getValueRecords()`: Returns the records for the field's current value.

- `getSubmitData()`: Allows submitting the field as a JSON encoded array.

Also the `BoxSelect` component provides the following two events for managing the selected items:

- valueSelectionChange

- valueFocusChange

Summary

In this chapter we've explored the features and also went through the usage of the `BoxSelect` combobox extension. We've learned how to configure the `BoxSelect` extension and its proper usage. We can see that by using Ext JS's extension feature we can easily use the full strength of the Ext JS library's `ComboBox` field and can add our own custom functionality to fulfill our needs.

Throughout this book we have learned the fundamentals of Ext JS plugins and extensions, we have introduced some of the popular Ext JS libraries and community provided plugins and extensions, and we have also provided several hands-on real world plugins and extensions development with proper explanations and code. We now have clear knowledge about the proper usage and development of Ext JS plugins and extensions.

Index

Thank you for buying
Ext JS 4 Plugin and Extension Development

About Packt Publishing

Packt, pronounced 'packed', published its first book "*Mastering phpMyAdmin for Effective MySQL Management*" in April 2004 and subsequently continued to specialize in publishing highly focused books on specific technologies and solutions.

Our books and publications share the experiences of your fellow IT professionals in adapting and customizing today's systems, applications, and frameworks. Our solution based books give you the knowledge and power to customize the software and technologies you're using to get the job done. Packt books are more specific and less general than the IT books you have seen in the past. Our unique business model allows us to bring you more focused information, giving you more of what you need to know, and less of what you don't.

Packt is a modern, yet unique publishing company, which focuses on producing quality, cutting-edge books for communities of developers, administrators, and newbies alike. For more information, please visit our website: www.packtpub.com.

About Packt Open Source

In 2010, Packt launched two new brands, Packt Open Source and Packt Enterprise, in order to continue its focus on specialization. This book is part of the Packt Open Source brand, home to books published on software built around Open Source licences, and offering information to anybody from advanced developers to budding web designers. The Open Source brand also runs Packt's Open Source Royalty Scheme, by which Packt gives a royalty to each Open Source project about whose software a book is sold.

Writing for Packt

We welcome all inquiries from people who are interested in authoring. Book proposals should be sent to author@packtpub.com. If your book idea is still at an early stage and you would like to discuss it first before writing a formal book proposal, contact us; one of our commissioning editors will get in touch with you.

We're not just looking for published authors; if you have strong technical skills but no writing experience, our experienced editors can help you develop a writing career, or simply get some additional reward for your expertise.

Learning Ext JS 4

ISBN: 978-1-84951-684-6   Paperback: 434 pages

Sencha Ext JS for a beginner

1. Learn the basics and create your first classes

2. Handle data and understand the way it works, create powerful widgets and new components

3. Dig into the new architecture defined by Sencha and work on real world projects

---

Instant Ext JS Starter [Instant]

ISBN: 978-1-78216-610-8   Paperback: 56 pages

Find out what Ext JS actually is, what you can do with it, and why it's so great

1. Learn something new in an Instant!
   A short, fast, focused guide delivering immediate results

2. Install and set up the environment with this quick Starter guide

3. Learn the basics of the framework and built-in utility functions

4. Use MVC architecture, components, and containers

Please check **www.PacktPub.com** for information on our titles

Mastering Ext JS

ISBN: 978-1-78216-400-5   Paperback: 358 pages

Learn how to build powerful and professional applications by mastering the Ext JS framework

1. Build an application with Ext JS from scratch

2. Learn expert tips and tricks to make your web applications look stunning

3. Create professional screens such as login, menus, grids, tree, forms, and charts

Sencha Architect App Development

ISBN: 978-1-78216-981-9   Paperback: 120 pages

Develop your own Ext JS and Sencha Touch application using Sencha Architect

1. Use Sencha Architect's features to improve productivity

2. Create your own application in Ext JS and Sencha Touch

3. Simulate, build, package and deploy your application using Sencha Command and Sencha Architect

www.ingramcontent.com/pod-product-compliance
Lightning Source LLC
Chambersburg PA
CBHW060157060326
40690CB00018B/4150